DOING BUSINESS IN ASIA

A HEAD START TO SUCCESS

DEVIN SPER

DOING BUSINESS IN ASIA
By Devin Sper

Copyright © 2022 by Devin Sper

All rights reserved.

No part of this book may be reproduced in any form or by any electronic or mechanical means, including information storage and retrieval systems, without written permission from the author, except for the use of brief quotations in a book review.

CONTENTS

Preface   v

1. INTRODUCTION TO ASIAN
BUSINESS CULTURE   1
How do Asians see us?   7

2. ASIA BUSINESS TRAVEL SECRETS   9
Free Hawaiian stopover   9
Dress well   12
Pack light   13
Business Class   15
Arrive in the evening   16
The Executive Floor   18
Skip lunch   20

3. SOURCING ASIAN PRODUCTS   23

4. CHINA   29
Historical Summary   29
Economy   32
People   33
Business customs   36
Beijing Hotels   42
Free Time   44
Recommended reading   50

5. HONG KONG   51
Historical Summary   51
Economy   53
People   55
Business customs   57

Hotels	58
Free Time	61
Recommended reading	65
6. JAPAN	67
Historical Summary	67
Economy	74
People	75
Business customs	79
Tokyo Hotels	83
Free Time	84
Recommended reading	85
7. TAIWAN	87
Historical Summary	87
Economy	90
People	91
Business customs	93
Taipei Hotels	94
Free Time	95
Recommended reading	100
Closing	101
Please consider leaving a review	103
About the Author	105

PREFACE

Having recently sold my company, Sper Scientific, and retired, I would like to share what I've learned during almost 40 years of doing business in Asia. I offer you my experience so that you may save yourself all the time and money I spent acquiring it. I will, for example, show you how to shortcut the years it took me to build my product line and do so in a matter of days! I will warn you of common mistakes that can permanently destroy a business relationship in Asia, and simple things that will instantly bring the relationship to a new level.

I will share things that will make your business trips more productive such as how staying on an executive floor can save you significant time and money and I will show you how to make your business trips more fun by, for example, enjoying a free Hawaiian vacation on every return trip from Asia.

Most of my advice revolves around Asian business culture and relationships and is relevant whether you work for a large company or are an entrepreneur starting from scratch, as I was. This book is relevant whether you are meeting your Asian business partners virtually or in person.

Doing business in Asia, or anywhere for that matter, is fundamentally different than being a tourist, and in my experience much more interesting. In business you interact with locals in a way tourists never do. In order to succeed, you must understand the local mindset and consider their interests. This requires you to know the people, where they come from (i.e. their history), the business culture and the current state of their economy.

I recommend everyone read the next two chapters: "Introduction to Doing Business in Asia" and "Asian Business Travel Secrets." If you intend to import products from Asia read the next chapter "Sourcing Asian Products" as well. The remaining chapters focus on individual countries and contain the following:

- Historical Summary – A brief history of the country emphasizing those aspects of its history relevant to the business culture.
- People – The nature of the people which differs greatly from one Asia country to the next.
- Business Customs – Specific to the particular country rather than to Asia as a whole.
- Hotels – My favorite hotels in the four main cities I am most familiar with and the reasons I recommend them. There are plenty

of other good hotels but these are ones I prefer and have regularly stayed at with particular advantages for business.
- Free Time – You will have free time the day of your arrival in each city and may also find yourself in Asia over a weekend. I'll offer you some fun and interesting things to do that you may not find in a typical tourist travel book.
- Books - Including historical novels, which are enjoyable reads for the flight over that offer insight into the culture.

Feel free to skip to your country of interest and to refer to other country chapters as needed or skip any other sections not of interest. Alternatively, reading book in its entirety may provide a broader picture and useful information as there is overlap in business customs between these countries. In any case the book is not long. I wanted to offer the essentials for doing business in Asia while not wasting your time with fluff. Throughout the book I illustrate points through my personal experiences to make them memorable and the book a fun, entertaining read. I believe you will find it both valuable and enjoyable.

1

INTRODUCTION TO ASIAN BUSINESS CULTURE

While meeting with a supplier at the Taipei Electronics Exhibition I could not help but notice another American businessman loudly berating his supplier in the next booth. I had no idea whether or not the American businessman's anger was justified, but I did know that he was certain to fail in his aims and that he might very well never hear from that supplier again.

I knew this because by that time I had learned the importance of the concept of "Face" in Asian business and culture in general. Of course it is bad form in any culture to publicly humiliate someone, but an American supplier might well overlook rude behavior on the part of a valuable customer under the adage that "the customer is always right." This will not fly in Asia, where face is more important than money and where causing someone to lose face is unforgivable and will permanently destroy the relationship.

To illustrate this further: I once mentioned to a

longtime Japanese customer and friend that I enjoyed gardening and he asked me why. I thought about it and said: "perhaps for the peaceful solitude." My friend said "perhaps far from voice of woman." I told my friend that I was surprised to hear this since Japanese wives appeared to be so quiet. He replied: "Only outside the house." In other words, Japanese couples may also at times argue, but only in private, they will *never* do so in public, as this would result in a loss of Face.

A corollary to Face is the importance of being polite in Asian culture. Whereas in the U.S. we may admire someone who is bold and outspoken, this would not generally be the case in Asia and a rude person will be viewed as a "barbarian." This is particularly true in Japan about which we will learn more in that chapter.

I begin with these examples to emphasize a point: Knowing a few key things about Asian business culture will help you immeasurably in doing business in Asia and not knowing these key things may well cause you to fail. Now I don't want to overstate my case, people are people and American businessmen sometimes make the opposite mistake imagining Asians so exotic they fail to relate to their Asian contacts on a basic human level. You do not have to become an expert in Asian culture to do business there, but a little understanding of, and sensitivity to, Asian business culture will go a long way towards insuring your success. Consider the interests and sensibilities of your Asian business partners, as well as your own, and they will do likewise.

More than that it will make your business in Asia exciting, enjoyable and broaden you as a person. I have developed many wonderful friendships which continue to this day. My annual trip to Asia was something I looked forward to all year. I brought my wife and each of my two daughters with me on various trips and they all had wonderful experiences they will never forget. Asians generally are very hospitable, enjoy showing guests from overseas around their hometowns, and they treated my family like royalty.

In Asian and Chinese culture in particular family is extremely important. Once while waiting to meet a Taiwanese supplier for lunch in my hotel lobby I stepped into the gift shop and ended up buying two necklaces made of small bits of aquamarine that looked like crushed ice. My supplier asked whom I had purchased them for and I explained that they were for my daughters Keren and Sivan. My supplier said, "yes family is the most important thing," and I could see that he respected me for feeling likewise.

Family is a universal human value and a very simple way to humanize yourself to your Asian contacts and visa versa. On my first business trip to Asia I was taken to lunch by a group of young people from a new supplier in Taiwan. Everything was business as usual until I happened to mention something about my family. My hosts became very interested, asked a lot of questions and then asked to see photos, which I showed them. Our relationship instantly deepened.

Most of my Asian business friends met my wife and daughters when they accompanied me on visits. They know all about them and always ask how they are doing. We do not see each other merely as foreign business people but as fathers, mothers, husbands and wives, as someone we can relate to.

I have become a great admirer of both Chinese and Japanese culture, which has both enriched my life and helped me in business. For example: I had developed a business relationship with a company in Beijing for a few years. Following one of my annual visits the owner, a kind young man named Zhong Hai, was taking me back to Beijing airport. As we were loading my bags into his car a few large books of Chinese art I had hastily stuffed into my knapsack fell out. Zhong Hai asked if I liked Chinese art. I explained that I had always loved art but had not understood Chinese art until my prior stop in Taipei. While there, a Taiwanese business friend had taken me to the National Palace Museum where they had a special exhibition on the Chinese artist Chang Dai-chien, (more about this amazing museum in the Chapter on Taiwan). With my friend's help I had begun to understand and appreciate Chinese art, and Chang Dai-chien in particular and purchased a few books of his art.

It turns out that Zhong Hai's grandfather was an artist who knew Chang Dai-chien and that Zhong Hai also loved art and was an intellectual. Now up until that point we had seen each other merely as business people but from that moment on we recognized each other as multi-dimensional human beings with shared interests and we became fast friends. I have been to his house, met his family and he has met mine He has taken me to interesting places around Beijing I would never have seen on my own and we have helped each other in many ways both business and personal. We became his company's exclusive agent and I knew that I could trust our agreement and Zhong Hai implicitly because our relationship went beyond mere business. Such relationships are invaluable. As a Taiwanese supplier once told me: "If you are in it only for the money you cannot make money." I would add conversely, that if you if you love what you are doing, the money will flow your way.

The author (left) with Zhong Hai.

I have learned a great deal from the wisdom of my Asian business friends and have even successfully applied some of these lessons to the American side of my business, something I believe gave me a competitive advantage. For example: Asian suppliers generally do not give out free samples of products even to important and well established customers, you want a sample you pay for it. Asian business culture is polite and respectful but no-nonsense.

Following standard business practice in the U.S. I

initially sent product samples free of charge to U.S. distributors who requested them following a sales call. More often than not, the distributor could not find the sample when I called to follow-up, and I had to send another then wait another week or two to follow-up again. People simply do not value free things. This problem magically disappeared once I switched to the Asian practice of billing for all samples. With an invoice addressed to his company attached to the sample my contact at the distributor had to account for it and always knew where the product was. Nor would he request the product in the first place if they were not seriously interested in it. This saved me valuable time and money especially when Sper Scientific was a struggling start-up.

Asian businesses rarely give their overseas customers credit terms such as net 30 days as is common in the United States. All shipments from are Asia must be paid for in advance, which generally means you pay upon placing the order. Asian manufacturers prefer to work on tight margins but take no monetary risk. The Asian manufacturer uses your money to purchase the materials and manufacture the goods. As a result it can take three to six months including shipping until you receive the goods and begin selling them. You have essentially given the manufacturer an interest free loan and are out the funds for all that time. The trade-off is a high profit margin on your end when you ultimately sell the product.

As my Asian suppliers got to know and trust me over time I was able to pay when goods were ready to ship, rather than payment upon order. This shortened the time we had to advance the funds by 3 to 6 months while still eliminating the supplier's risk. This would not have been possible without the close personal relationships I developed with my Asian partners.

How do Asians see us?

On the plus side Asian business friends describe Americans as happy, optimistic, free-spirited, non-threatening, easy to talk to, open, confident, highly-efficient, direct and honest. One Taiwanese friend notes that she has never been asked for an under the table commission by an American. My longtime Chinese friend Zhong Hai, agrees that there is "no B.S" with Americans. This direct "yes or no" approach however is not viewed favorably by everyone. Some Asians, like Zhong Hai, appreciate it while others find it cold and impersonal. A Japanese business friend complains that Americans are too concerned with performance rather than building long-term relationships.

Another complaint I've heard is that American companies do not invest in training the way European companies do, resulting in rapid turnover in employees. This is a problem when doing business in Asia where building personal relationships are so key.

Zhong Hai tells me that the Chinese people worship foreign things and particularly American culture and I have seen evidence of this throughout Asia. In Japan for example, I saw billboards for American brands, with English slogans that makes no sense and I've seen Japanese wearing T-shirts with the same sort of nonsensical English. My Japanese business friend explained that Japanese consider English slogans cool and are unconcerned with their meaning, as most do not understand the language anyway. In Asia, as throughout the world, modern culture is imitative of Western and particularly American culture although each country puts its own spin on it.

Zhong Hai goes on to say that five or six years ago the United States was the most admired country among the Chinese but more recently, the Chinese government has played up hostility from the U.S. towards China. Until recently most Chinese were simple farmers and believe what their government is telling them: That the U.S. government wants to control and conquer China and this has created a strong antagonism towards the United States.

On a personal level however, the Chinese remain kind, curious and full of admiration for Americans they meet. You will encounter no animosity from the Chinese as long as you avoid politics. In particular, do not lecture Chinese about the superiority of the American political system, American values, or Americans as a people as some do in a condescending way. I think this is good advice anywhere in Asia, or anywhere in the world for that matter.

2
ASIA BUSINESS TRAVEL SECRETS

Free Hawaiian stopover

On one of my annual trips to Asia my travel agent, Dave, booked me on a connection via Honolulu, rather than on the West Coast as usual. He did this simply because it happened to be the least expensive route. It turns out that Hawaiian flights from both the U.S. and Asia are primarily for tourists and therefore significantly less expensive than direct flights from the West Coast to Asia which are aimed primarily at business people. I asked Dave what would happen if I got off the plane in Honolulu and made the same connection a few days later and he said "nothing, the fare would remain the same." The airfare savings via Honolulu was over $1,000, which pretty much covered my hotel and restaurant expenses for a couple of days in Hawaii.

From then on I always stopped in Honolulu on my way back from Asia. While the business trips to Asia were fun and exciting they were also mentally and physically exhausting. You have a full schedule of important meetings, are on the whole time, focused on the business at hand and anxious to make a good impression. Doing this with a 16-hour time difference makes this even more difficult and 35 hours of flying in 10 days also takes its toll. While enjoying my time in Asia I always looked forward to relaxing in Hawaii, especially towards the end of the trip and fell asleep each night in Asia happily anticipating it.

There are non-stop flights to Hawaii from both Tokyo and Beijing so I would arrange my Asian trips to end up in one of those two cities. I always flew Hawaiian Airlines, not because it was necessarily the best airline, but because it allowed me to begin my vacation while still on the tarmac in Asia. You feel the decompression immediately on boarding. The aircrafts' interior is decorated Hawaiian style and the crew welcomes you dressed in Aloha shirts and flowers. The monitors play videos of beautiful Hawaiian waterfalls while soothing Hawaiian music plays on the speakers. By the time you sit down and preview the magazines and menu covered with pictures of Hawaii you have left business behind and are already on your Hawaiian vacation.

After dinner had been cleared and the lights dimmed I would take a sleeping pill. I do not take them regularly but they are great for long overseas flights. They help you adjust to the time zone, and enable you to arrive fresh and well-rested. Since you sleep deeply and without interruption the next thing you know you have been magically transported 8 hours forward and the next thing you hear is "fasten your seatbelts" as you begin descending to Hawaii. I would slide open the shade and see the green mountains of Oahu in the distance. The flight from Asia always passes directly over Pearl Harbor. Take a seat on the passenger side of the plane and you will also have a great view as it passes parallel to Waikiki beach and Diamond Head.

I would take a taxi to my hotel, enjoy a meal, perhaps wander around a bit, and when it was time to go to bed invariably collapse and sleep soundly exhausted from the entire trip. It was always the most wonderful feeling awakening the next day to the view of Waikiki Beach and Diamond Head and realize I was now on vacation, free to relax and do whatever I pleased. It was as if God had placed Hawaii in the middle of the Pacific Ocean just for tired business travelers returning from Asia.

Waikiki beach from the Mona Surfrider, Honolulu.

Eventually it became even more fun when my wife began meeting me in Hawaii. Tanya would fly directly from the U.S. and whomever arrived first would wait for the other on the large porch in front porch of our favorite hotel the Moana Surfrider. The Moana was the first hotel on Waikiki which, in fact, developed around it, and has been restored to its original elegance. Entering the lobby is like stepping in to old Hawaii and the perfect beginning to my free Hawaiian vacation. Don't forget to book yours when buying your ticket to Asia.

Dress well

Asians dress for business like American's used to years ago with Japanese the most formal of all. Men usually wear a suit and women a suit or a dress. It's always a good idea to dress well on business but in Asia it is essential. I believe this holds true even for virtual meetings. I was once browsing a shop at Taipei airport prior to my departure. I was still wearing my business clothes but had removed my suit jacket and replaced it with a fitted sweater for the flight. The sales girl asked where I was from. When I told her I was an American she was surprised and said she had thought I was European. I asked why and she said in an agitated voice: "Because you aren't dressed like…a potato!"

I have always found a suit great for business travel. It makes packing simple and light as all you need carry in addition are underwear, socks, a tie and white shirts, (no worries about what goes with what). You already have pants and a jacket you can take it on and off as needed. Don't worry about it becoming creased in the carry-on. Before going to bed hang the suit it in your hotel room bathroom together with a white shirt for the next day. Run the shower hot for a few minutes until the bathroom steams up. Don't overdo it to where your clothes are soaking wet, and if you do just take them out of the bathroom and hang them in the closet. By the next morning your suit and shirt will look like it was pressed at the cleaners.

If you take my advice and wear a suit, invest in a good one as a bad suit is worse than none at all. I never had more than two suits at a time, one winter and one summer weight, but always quality. A quality wool suit that fits well, makes you look good and feel good about yourself. People treat you with respect when you wear a suit, not just in business but in hotels, stores, restaurants, taxis, everywhere you go. By the time you arrive at your meeting you feel like a million dollars and your self-confidence comes across and is winning.

Pack light

I'm sure you've heard this before but packing light and not having to drag heavy suitcases around the world is liberating. It is not only less tiring but avoids wasting time waiting for bags on arrival. More importantly you avoid lost bags, no fun as a tourist but a disaster on business trips.

Although a highly-rated airline, Singapore Air once lost my bag on the way to Asia. Actually they didn't lose it but it was a day behind me the entire trip which, for practical purposes, amounts to the same thing. I had never been to Singapore before and was hoping to spend my first day recovering from the trip and seeing something of the city, prior to business the next day. Instead, I had to run around the city looking for a suit, shoes, shirts, socks, a tie, everything, as I had only the crumpled clothes I'd slept in on the plane. I didn't have time to find things that fit really well and they would be redundant when I got home anyway. I had to pay for everything out of my own pocket since, technically, the airline hadn't lost my bags, they were just delayed and they only provided me with a wash kit. A great waste of time, energy and money. After that experience, I no longer checked bags but took only a carry-on for two weeks in Asia and will share with you a few simple tricks that will enable you to do likewise.

First of all, as mentioned above, packing a suit makes things simple. Secondly you can pack for only half the trip and simply have the hotel do laundry at the halfway point. Alternatively, save all your worn out socks and underwear for the trip and discard them after wearing. Your suitcase now becomes lighter as you travel and leaves room for anything you might purchase overseas. I also took a folding bag into which I could throw laundry at the end leaving the carry-on free, if needed, for gifts and other purchase. You need little or no wash kit as any decent Asian hotel room provides not only soap and shampoo as in the States but combs, toothbrushes, toothpaste and shavers as well. Now just take

Business Class

When I first began Sper Scientific I had little money and simply purchased the least expensive tourist class ticket available to Asia. One day the airline had empty seats in business class on my return flight from Tokyo and they bumped me up without my even asking, probably due to my high number of miles. The difference was night and day. I was in the bubble on the second floor of a 747 with a total of only 6 passengers and an equal number of flight attendants. The others passengers were all Japanese business men who expect the flight attendants to snap-to as would their Japanese employees. For my part I was happy to just relax and sleep after two exciting but intense weeks of business in Asia. Naturally all of the flight attendants wanted to be my server and thereby avoid the more demanding passengers

Needless to say the service I received was above and beyond anything I had experienced in economy class. After dinner one flight attendant asked why I had not eaten my dessert. I explained that I tried to eat healthy, that had it been something chocolate I might not have been able to resist but I could pass on the pudding, or whatever it was. A short time later she returned with a bowl of Godiva chocolates!

Later I decided to stretch my legs and began to descend the spiral staircase to the first floor economy section. It was like descending into hell, smoky (in those days smoking was still allowed) crowded, babies crying, people draped all over the seats. I never made it to the bottom of the staircase but simply reversed course midway and went back up to business class heaven.

Once I could afford to, I began flying business class on all flights to Asia and recommend you do the same as soon as you are able. Of course the food and service are better and the cabin less crowded but most importantly the seat folds down enabling you to get a good night's sleep and arrive in much better shape to do business.

Arrive in the evening

If possible I always tried to arrive in Asia in the early evening. It will be hard enough doing business with the 16 to 19-hour time difference (depending on where in North America you are starting from). Missing a full night's sleep makes it that much more difficult. No matter how young you are, or how well you slept on the plane, you will not be able to fully focus on business the day of your arrival due to the vast time difference. I once made the mistake of taking a flight that arrived in the morning and, even though I had the day free, it was torture trying to stay awake the whole day. Arriving in the early evening allows you time to get to your hotel, have dinner, unpack and get a good night's sleep. In the morning you'll be fresh and ready for business.

Although you'll fall asleep easily through sheer exhaustion you will probably pop up wide awake up in the middle of the night due to the extreme time difference. My solution was to have half a sleeping pill and a glass of water on my night table and take it at that point. A full Ambien gives me 7 to 8 hours of sleep. I sleep just as soundly with half a pill but for half the time, so about 4 hours and I've never experienced side effects. I do this for the first three days on arrival in Asia and then stop so as not to become addicted, then the same on my return home. Although the sleeping pill helps you adjust to the time difference more quickly after the 3 days I would still find myself wanting to sleep in the early evening and wake up very early. I've read that you need about one day to adjust for every time zone and have found that to be accurate. It will therefore take about two weeks on your return from Asia to fully adjust to the time difference. This does not happen all at once but gradually over time with your sleep schedule becoming a little more normal each day. In the meantime, just roll with it. Wake up early get washed and dressed, prepare for your meetings, eat breakfast as soon as the restaurant opens and before you know it will be time for business and you'll be ready to go.

Likewise, I recommend allowing a full day for travel between cities in Asia and avoid scheduling business for the same day. Even relatively short flights like Taiwan – Hong Kong take much of a day when you include check-out, check-in, travel to and from the airport and waiting for boarding. Delayed flights result in missed meetings.

Asian business partners will sometimes offer to pick

you up at the airport. I suggest avoiding this and taking a taxi instead. A Taiwanese supplier once arranged to pick me up at Taipei airport on my arrival from the United. States. The flight was many hours late and my poor friend had to wait around the airport all that time. Of course, being a typically polite Asian, he did not mention it, but I'm sure he was miserable and had better things to do with his time. On top of that I was still in the clothes I had put on over 20 hours earlier and slept in on the flight. All I could do was wash up as best I could in the airplane sink designed for contortionists. Much better to just take a taxi to your hotel as you are and crash with an entire night and morning the next day to rest and prepare for meetings.

The Executive Floor

Many business hotels have executive floor but those in the United States are often just one or two guest room set aside for snacks and perhaps breakfast. Some Asian hotels however, have special floors built for this purpose with a concierge stationed in a common lounge area in the center of the floor, usually the top floor. These can be well worth the higher room price if you use them, as I have, for meetings.

Most of my key suppliers exhibited at a series of electronics trade shows held one after another, each October, throughout Asia. I always scheduled my Asian trip accordingly and was able to meet many suppliers on a single day as they all had booths at the same show. There were however, other companies, often smaller but still important to our business, who did not exhibit at the shows. Rather than spending days running around the country for meetings at their offices or factories I scheduled back-to-back meetings at my executive lounge and met them all in a single day. This saves many hotel nights and more than pays for the extra cost of an executive floor room.

I would give the executive floor concierge a schedule of my appointments and as each arrived the concierge would greet them, ask them to be seated in one of the comfortable couches or chairs and call my room. In this way the concierge acts as your executive assistant would in an office. I would then come out to the lounge for the meeting. Good executive floors not only serve meals but have coffee, tea, drinks and snacks throughout the day, which I was able to offer to my business partners as well.

You may be thinking: Why can't I save the extra charge for an executive floor room and just hold meetings in my room or in the regular hotel lobby on the ground floor? Both are bad ideas. Meeting in your room means you will have to straighten it up prior to each meeting and it will still not be fresh. There may be only one chair so someone will have to sit on the bed with no work table between you. Not a professional atmosphere or the way you want to present yourself.

The main downstairs lobby is usually noisy, crowded and lacking privacy, not a good place for a productive meeting. By contrast a meeting on the executive floor lounge is quiet, professional and civilized. You can leave your room as is, since your visitors are not going to see it.

Many business-oriented hotels have business or conference rooms that you can rent by the hour. However, these will cost you far more than the extra charge for an executive floor room and they do not come with refreshments and a concierge. Nobody will inform you as your appointments arrive so you will have to spend the whole day in the conference room rather than relaxing in yours between meetings, some of which may show up late, or not at all.

Additional benefits are fast check in and out in with your concierge in the quiet executive lounge, rather than waiting on line in the lobby, very welcome after you've traveled for many hours. The concierge will also take care of any further travel arrangements you need to make on the fly, which they are much better equipped to do since they speak the language, leaving you free to focus on business.

Skip lunch

In Asia, as in Europe, breakfast is included in the room rate. If you are staying on the executive floor, breakfast will be served in the lounge area while other guests will be served in one of the hotel restaurants. Either way Asian hotel breakfasts are tremendous buffets featuring Western, Japanese and Chinese breakfast food as well as fresh juices, coffee, all types of bread pastry, cheeses, spreads desserts and more. Cooks will also make eggs or cut a side of meat to your order.

As I've mentioned before Asians are generally very hospitable and you will likely receive one or more invitations to dinner during the day. These are usually incredible meals; some were the best in my life. Everyone sits around a table with a large lazy Susan on to which the servers will place an endless supply of wonderful dishes. Your hosts will insist you try everything and additional main courses will be brought directly to you.

Beijing Duck

On one such occasion in Beijing the food was wonderful but I simply could not eat another bite. I thought the meal was finally over when my hosts told me the servers would soon bring roast pig for the main course. This was my out as I explained that, for religious reasons, I do not eat pork. My hosts really couldn't argue with that and said something to the servers. I thanked God for making me a Jew and felt I had dodged a bullet. You can imagine my consternation when, a while later they brought out roast lamb!

What I did not yet know was that, as long as you are eating, the food will continue coming as your hosts will assume you may still be hungry despite your protests to the contrary. You simply have to stop eating if you don't want to explode. My other suggestion is to skip lunch. That way you can truly enjoy the terrific breakfast buffet and dinners which are more than enough. You'll feel better while spending virtually nothing on food for your entire trip. If you want something in between and are staying on the executive floor, there are always the free snacks in the lounge which in some hotels are more like a full meal.

3

SOURCING ASIAN PRODUCTS

If you are seeking to import products from Asia, I can suggest a number of resources that will enable you to quickly locate potential suppliers.

The fastest way to find suppliers is to visit trade shows in your field. At the right show you can, in a single day, collect catalogs for later review, and contact dozens of potential suppliers. The suppliers will have all their products on display at their booth so you can see them demonstrated and ask questions. Equally important you will meet the marketing staff and often the company president. You can introduce yourself and begin the personal relationship with them that is so important, something you cannot do through correspondence alone. The annual electronics shows I attended were timed sequentially so that you could visit each country's one after the other. When I started Sper Scientific I developed my product line through correspondence alone as I felt I could not yet afford the trip to Asia. In hindsight it would have saved me years building my product line, and been far less expensive had I visited the appropriate trade shows right away.

The author (right) with a supplier at the H.K. Electronics Exhibition.

In addition, most countries have a government office dedicated to helping their exporters and happy to help you connect with them. These offices are often the trade show organizers. Those relevant to the countries we are covering are listed below:

Hong Kong Trade Development Corporation (HKTDC) organizes many of the H.K. shows. They publish, and will be happy to send you, sleek color magazines each full of appropriate products for specific fields: electronics, medical devices, housewares, etc. You also can review digital copies as well as find trade shows, connect with potential suppliers on their website: www.hktdc.com or contact HKTDC directly for help in finding one.

Taiwan External Trade Development Council (TAITRA) operates the Taipei Convention Center and organizes many of Taiwan's shows. To encourage attendance at the Taipei Electronics Show their LA office (they have 60 branches worldwide) would send me an invitation each year and actually pay for my airfare and hotel. Like HKTDC they also publish magazines full of products for specific fields. You also can find trade shows and find and connect with potential suppliers on their website: https://en.taitra.org.tw or contact TAITRA directly for help in finding one.

Japan External Trade Organization (JETRO) is more focused on supporting Japanese companies and investment in specific fields and markets but you can contact them with any product enquires you have **www.jetro.go.jp/en/**

Two other good, business-to-business websites for sourcing Asian products are:

- Global Sources: www.globalsources.com
- Made in China: www.made-in-china.com

I should note that finding a supplier is one thing. Qualifying a supplier and product quality control is an entirely different story. Although not the subject of this book here in a nutshell is a simple and effective method I used:

First I would do an initial market research which

consisted of looking at what was currently on the market and to see if the product under consideration had any advantages in function and/or price and then create a comparison table.

If the product looked promising on paper, we ordered one sample. If the sample tested well, we ordered ten more. If *all* ten tested well, we ordered 100 samples. At each stage we made clear to the supplier that we intended to test 100% of the samples. If, knowing this, the supplier could not send us properly working samples, we did not pursue the matter further.

If all these tested well, we placed a larger OEM (Original Equipment Manufacturer) order with our product and packaging design. On initial orders with a new supplier we tested 100% of these as well. Only after the first large order passed Q.C. and was in stock would we introduce the product. For subsequent shipments we referenced standard A.Q.L. (Acceptable Quality Limit) inspection sampling, making allowances for our confidence level in the supplier based on previous shipments.

Since all orders from Asia, including samples, are paid for in advance this method minimizes risk and saves time in the long-run. Receiving a few bad samples is far less expensive and time consuming than investing in, shipping, inspecting, and ultimately rejecting a large order with an unacceptable level of defectives. It is infinitely better than shipping out bad product which will disappoint your customers and being forced to deal with customer returns. It also puts the supplier on notice that you are serious about quality. Knowing we would test and return defective products our suppliers were generally careful about what they shipped us. They preferred to send questionable product elsewhere.

4

CHINA

Historical Summary

China is one of the world's great civilizations and one of the oldest with written records dating back to 1250 BC. The cradle of Chinese civilization began along the Yellow and Yangtze rivers which was eventually consolidated under the Shang Dynasty.

Under the Tang Dynasty (618 to 907 A.D.) China invented gunpowder and used it in warfare for the first time. Under the Song Dynasty (960 – 1279 AD), Chinese civilization become the most technologically advanced in the world. The compass was invented enabling China to build large ocean going ships for trade and the first Chinese Navy. The economy prospered, and China issued the world's first paper currency. China's cities became the largest in the world and the total population surpassed 100 million.

In the 15th century China built trading ships of over 1,500 tons. By comparison a Portuguese carvel of the same era was 130 tons and Europe would not build ships as large for many centuries. Fleets of these large "treasure ships," traded across the Indian Ocean as far as Africa. However, fearing foreign corruption, the treasure fleets were abandoned and China cut off trade with the outside world in 1424 A.D.

This happened at the very same time that Europe was beginning the age of discovery and it is for these reasons that Europe advanced technologically while China stagnated and fell behind. Between 1839 to 1912 the European colonial powers forced China to sign a series of humiliating treaties giving them control of China's ports in order that they might exploit China economically and control its trade. China has never forgotten this humiliation and exploitation and this is key to understanding current Chinese foreign policy.

After ruling China for 450 years the final Qing Dynasty was overthrown in 1912 in a popular revolt led by intellectuals, most prominent among them being Sun Yat-sen, and was replaced by the Republic of China. The country was determined to modernize without abandoning Chinese culture, but united by little else and a period of chaos ensued. Following Sun Yat-sen's death in 1925, a fourteen year long civil war broke out between the Communists led by Mao Tse-Tung and the Nationalists led by Chiang Kai Shek. The two armies continued to fight each other, as well as the Japanese occupiers, until the end of World War II in 1945.

During their occupation (1937 to 1945) the Japanese not only exploited China economically, as had the Europeans, but exhibited extreme cruelty towards the Chinese. In the city of Nanjing alone as many as 300,000 Chinese were murdered and 80,000 women raped.

Following Japan's defeat bloodshed continued for another four years between the Nationalists and Communists. Eventually the Communists gained control of the mainland and founded the PRC (People's Republic of China) while the Nationalists established the ROC (Republic of China) on the Island of Taiwan. Both entities remain in place today. (For more on Taiwan see the Historical summary in the Chapter "Taiwan").

In heavy handed Communist style Mao's government forcibly collectivized land ownership and modernized industry while 45 million people were executed or starved to death in "The Great Leap Forward." In 1966 Mao began his Cultural Revolution resulting in ten more years of terror.

In 1972 tension with the Soviet Union led China to open a working relationship with the United States under President Richard Nixon. The United States, along with most of the world, now recognized the PRC, previously treated as a pariah, as the sole legitimate government of China and seated it in place of the ROC at the United Nations.

After a power struggle following Mao's death in 1976, Deng Xiaoping emerged as the new leader of China and instituted economic reforms that privatized much of the Chinese economy. Demanding political reforms protests broke out in Tiananmen Square and elsewhere and continued for several months before being brutally repressed. In 2001 China joined the World Trade Organization opening the door to her rapid, export-driven, economic boom, modernization and urbanization.

In 2012 Xi Jinping ascended to power, dispensing with collective leadership and beginning a new era in the history of the PRC. He began consolidating power internally by instituting an anti-corruption campaign, tightening his control of the State and state control of the economy and ending term limits. He appointed himself commander-in-chief of the military and instituting a cult of personality around himself reminiscent of Mao Tse-Tung.

President Xi's overarching goal is for China to replace the United States as the preeminent world power. To this end Xi has allied himself with fellow authoritarians Vladimir Putin of Russia, North Korea's Kim Jung-un, and Iran's Ayatollah Khamenei all of whom seek to undermine America's position in the world and establish a new authoritarian world order.

Economy

China today has a GDP of 17.7 trillion dollars, second only to the U.S. GDP of 23 trillion. China is the world's largest exporter, largest manufacturer and the world's largest e-commerce market. It is the second largest retail market overall with the largest middle class in the world and the highest number of billionaires Private industry accounts for most of the economy but the state retains control of key energy and heavy industries.

Key to achieving President's Xi's goal of surpassing the U.S is China's Belt and Road initiative. This program seeks to have China replace the U.S. atop the world's supply chain by creating a modern Silk Road across Eurasia with China as its core. China has signed Belt and Road agreements with seventy countries and is investing 50 to 100 billion dollars per year in building transportation and other infrastructure across the region in order to integrate their economies with China's.

Another aspect of Xi's strategy is the "Made in China 2025" initiative which targets and invests in key technology sectors with the goal of surpassing the United States technologically. Prior to 2018 these policies were generally ignored outside of China. Under President Trump the United States began to push back against unfair Chinese trade practices, and industrial espionage. Tariffs were imposed on most Chinese products to counter long-standing Chinese tariffs on U.S. products. Under the Biden administration the United States has largely reverted to the previous U.S. policy of ignoring the issue.

People

China is the most populous country in the world with over 1.4 billion people, 90% of whom are ethnic "Han" Chinese. That is about four times the population of the United States in roughly the same land area. Although China's many regions each have their own language or dialect, today Mandarin is the official language of China and primary language of business.

Until fairly recently China was a poor country and the Chinese suffered immensely throughout their history from both poverty and oppression. Suffering has instilled in the Chinese people a depth of character and empathy for other people and they are generally warm, interested in other cultures, and tolerant. In comparison to the U.S., violent crime is rare in China, even in the large cities.

Chinese are individualists by nature although Confucian ethics keeps this more in check than among Americans. They are also ambitious, and entrepreneurial, seeing life as a great adventure and to take it as far as they can go. Some take this to an extreme opening the door to corruption.

The Chinese are intelligent problem solvers who can think outside the box. One morning at a meeting in Beijing I mentioned that some of the plastic vials of calibration solution we included with each product leaked. One man immediately left the meeting and did not return until the afternoon at which time he bought a non-leaking vial having already fixed the problem on the production line. In the U.S., Europe or Japan this would have taken numerous meetings, engineering drawings and correspondence over weeks, if not months.

The best way I can describe the Chinese is that they are a lot like Americans, and in some ways more like Americans used to be. Chinese have not lost touch with their ancient culture and history. They know who they are, where they come from, and where they are headed. Even those that do not necessarily support the Communist government are patriotic and rightfully proud of their country's achievements. The family unit is strong in China, and central to their world. They respect their elders and dote on their children whose education is of primary importance. Nobody has ever accused the Chinese of being lazy and their work ethic is well-known.

Unlike the other Western powers, the United States did not participate in the Western occupation of China and opposed it, seeking free trade instead. During World War II the U.S. was China's key ally in her struggle against the common Japanese enemy. Despite the hostility of China's current Communist regime towards the United States, the Chinese people remain favorably disposed towards America and all that she stands for. This was dramatically displayed during the massive 1989 protests when the protesters erected a huge model of the Statue of Liberty in Tiananmen Square in the heart of Beijing. As an American I've never experienced anything but great warmth and admiration for the United States of America from the Chinese people.

I have watched China go from an under-developed country to a superpower and am not surprised by it. I believe China has achieved this success on the strength of her traditional values and culture and despite Communist rule rather than because of it. I also believe that if the U.S. must have a rival on the world stage, as seems inevitable, I would rather it was China than

Germany, Russia, Japan, the Islamic world or almost any other potential rival. Not because I am fond of the current Chinese government but because the Chinese as a people are generally non-violent, pragmatic, kind, decent and primarily focused on bettering their lives and I believe this must ultimately be reflected in their country's policies.

With Sivan in Beijing

Business customs

For decades, following the Communist takeover of China in 1949, the country remained economically undeveloped and impoverished. Communist attempts to force economic progress through central government mandates and terror set the country back even further with tens of millions of people starving to death during

Mao's "Great Leap Forward." The situation became so desperate that the government eventually began to tolerate and encourage free market initiatives. This eventually became government policy in the 1980s under Deng Xiaoping. The result was the explosion in Chinese manufacturing and export that we now see dominating world markets. Although the Communist Party of China still rules the country the economy today is largely free market with large numbers of private enterprises large and small. Keep in mind however, that China is not a democracy and avoid politics as your partner may be reluctant to express his true opinion.

China's adoption of capitalist economics was so rapid and wildly successful because the Chinese people are by nature entrepreneurs. Once in China I brought knock-off pocketbooks as gifts for my wife, daughters and female friends which turned out to be a big hit. At that time the knock-offs were very inexpensive, (not anymore), so luckily I bought more than one for each. This turned out to be fortuitous since they loved some and not others. On my next trip I asked my daughter Keren to cut out a magazine ad for the pocketbook she wanted.

When I got to Beijing I went to a market made up of many small booths selling luggage and pocketbooks. On entering I was immediately approached by a little girl who noticed Keren's magazine clipping of the pocketbook in my hand. She said: "Is this what you are looking for?" to which I answered: "yes." She said "what color? "I replied: "White, like in the ad." Without asking permission she grabbed the clippings from my hand and took off, returning after a while with a perfect replica of the white Chanel bag pictured in the ad. It wasn't a real Chanel but it was real leather and nicely made. After I bought it from her she said: "Do you want the matching wallet?" then produced it and sold me that too!

This little girl, who did not own a booth but probably knew each one by heart, took the initiative and within a few minutes made what I'm sure was a nice profit. She saved me the time and effort of finding it, (I probably would never have found that exact bag), so I was happy to pay her and my daughter was thrilled. Such initiative, entrepreneurial spirit and making something out of nothing is typically Chinese.

Once while visiting a factory making mercury laboratory thermometers I noticed a young woman whose job it was to sit and watch each thermometer as it came down the production line making sure the level of mercury was in line with a reference mark inscribed on a post directly in front of her. On leaving the factory hours later I noticed her seated in the same spot with her eyes still focused on the reference mark and mercury level of each thermometer as it came by.

This sort of self-discipline in a young employee would be hard to find in America today. Likewise, sobriety, an intact family structure and the ability to think on their feet is typical of the Chinese workforce and unfortunately no longer so typical of ours as it once was. In my opinion this sober, disciplined, intelligent workforce, entrepreneurial spirit and healthy society are more significant factors in China's economic rise and competitiveness, than the industrial espionage, or government policies to which Chinese success is often attributed in our media.

The underside of China's fast economic growth are the scams and corruption that often accompany a rapid rise to riches. China is like the wild west of business where the normal rules don't always apply. We have all read about the theft of intellectual property, currency manipulation and unfair trade practices to which the Chinese courts and government turn a blind eye.

As an importer of Chinese products I have not experienced more problems buying from China than other countries but have heard many horror stories from people seeking to sell to China. Some Chinese companies exploit the desire of foreign companies to enter the huge Chinese market by stringing them along, requesting bribes, and not delivering on their promises.

As I mentioned we generally purchased from, rather than sold to, China but occasionally received enquiries from Chinese customers seeking to buy one of our products on our website. One day we received a request for a proforma invoice from a customer in China for a large quantity of our most expensive product. I was naturally skeptical of so large an order from an unknown overseas buyer. However, the customer accompanied his request for quotation with on point technical questions on the product. More importantly the buyer agreed to our price and terms of payment which, for export orders, were always payment in advance. Since he agreed to send payment before we shipped the goods I couldn't see how we could lose on the transaction.

The buyer wrote that since this would be the first order of many he would like to meet me personally and asked that I come to China to accept the order. This was not an unreasonable request considering the size of the order and the importance Asians placed on personal relationships in business. The potential profit would more than cover the cost of the trip.

I had only just returned from Asia and was still tired from my travels. However, the employee who received the order, had never been to Asia and was anxious to go so I sent him. He quickly arranged flights and a hotel to Zhengzhou where the customer was located. On the morning following his arrival our man was met in his hotel lobby by two young women whom he expected were going to take him to the company. Instead they told him that it was traditional to bring a gift and that they would take him shopping to buy one for the boss. Our employee now became skeptical and contacted me. I told him that a small symbolic gift was ok but something valuable was inappropriate. The girls brought him directly to a store selling gold and said that "The boss likes gold" and insisted that he buy a gold bar. Realizing we'd been had he refused and returned to Phoenix on the earliest possible flight.

Afterwards I told my friend Zhong Hai about the incident and he replied that Zhengzhou and Henan province in which it was located were poor areas and known as the scam capital of China. As the Chinese say "out of poverty comes evil water." I then googled

Zhengzhou and it popped right up as a scam city. We would have saved ourselves considerable time and money had I done this, or asked my friend Zhong Hai, in the first place but the thought never occurred to me.

This and similar scams are not limited to Henan and abound all over China and I know people who have encountered more elaborate scams than this. In another common scam the Chinese partner negotiated an exclusivity contract by claiming to have distribution and connections he did not have and never delivered on his side of the agreement.

Again, I have not encountered any such scams importing Chinese products and found the Chinese to be no more or less honest than business people elsewhere. These sort of scams are generally perpetrated on companies seeking to export to China. This does not mean you can't make money selling to China, many companies do, but you must be cautious and do your due diligence regarding your potential Chinese partners.

The first step is to verify that your supplier is in fact a manufacturer and not some sort of agent or reseller. Many Chinese companies who present themselves as such but are actually some sort of reseller. The best way to do this is to visit the factory (not the office), prior to placing your first large order. I know of one case in which the Chinese set up an entire fake company office to fool an American visitor. At the factory you want to do three things:

1. See the production line.

2. Have the Q.C. process explained to you. At this stage it doesn't matter what their Q.C. process is, the point is to confirm that they have one.
3. Meet the boss and begin to establish a personal relationship with him. This can often be done over lunch, or better yet dinner. The Chinese are by nature shy but having a meal and drink together usually breaks the ice. If possible he is the one you want to correspond with in the future.

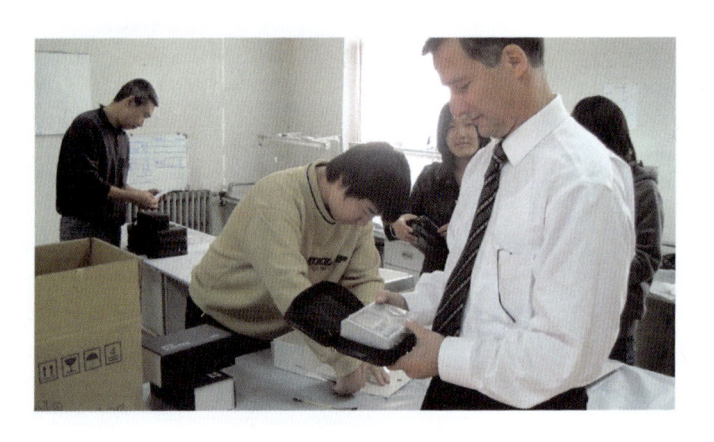

The author at a factory in Beijing.

Beijing Hotels

Beijing is one of the largest cities in the world so the hotel you choose will depend on where you have business, and the sights you want to see. Whatever area of the city you visit you are guaranteed to find a large selection of hotels in every price range. As is generally the case in Asia, most Beijing business hotels offer service above and beyond what we are used to in the States. Here are a few I've stayed in and recommend:

Grand Hyatt is an excellent modern Western style business hotel located in the center of Beijing, walking distance to the main tourist sights which are all adjacent to each other: The Forbidden City, Palace Museum, Tiananmen Square, Jingshan Park, Beihai Park and the Houhai Bar Street nightlife area. The Grand Hyatt has an amazing underground indoor pool built to resemble a tropical paradise, complete with tropical plants, rock waterfalls, warm fragrant air, jungle sounds, lounge chairs and an illuminated ceiling with stars. It is so well done you can forget you are indoors. Just next to the pool is a good hotel gym. The Grand Hyatt Beijing is adjacent to a gigantic high end shopping mall with 600 stores on three levels. The mall has an extensive restaurant court built around an atrium where you will find many types of food and better value than the typically very overpriced restaurants in high end Chinese hotels.

Grand Hyatt Beijing
Address: 1 East Chang An Avenue, Beijing China, 100738
Email: Beijing.grand@hyatt.com
Website: www.hyatt.com/en-US/hotel/china/grand-hyatt-beijing/beigh

Shangri-La Hotel in the North West Haidan District is Chinese elegance, a peaceful retreat from the crowds and traffic of Beijing. The hotel features an idyllic Chinese garden with covered walkways modeled on the nearby Summer Palace one of Beijing's main sights and certainly worth a visit.

Shangri-La Hotel, Beijing
Address: 29 Zizhyuan Road, Beijing China, 1000089,
Email: sib@Shangri-La.com
Website: www.shangri-la.com/Beijing/shangrila

East Hotel is an ultra-modern business hotel in the North East not too far from the airport but quite far from the main tourist sites in the city center. I have stayed at this hotel and held meetings here to avoid spending hours in Beijing's terrible traffic in and out of the city center.

East Hotel Beijing
No. 22 Jiuxiaqiao Road, Chaoyang Disrict, Beijing China, 100016
Email: answers@-east-beijing.com
Website: www.easthotels.com/sc/beijing

Free Time

If you have time one evening, and want to see something uniquely Chinese and a lot of fun I recommend attending a performance of Chinese Opera. Even if you don't care for Western Opera you may be surprised how much fun Chinese Opera is, which, despite the name, is something entirely different. The stage settings are simple, perhaps nothing more than a curtain, everything else however, is over the top exaggeration.

The costumes and make up are incredibly elaborate takes on traditional Chinese clothing with different colors and elements indicating the status and nature of the character. I remember one female actress had little puff balls on springs projecting out of her headdress. As is typical in Chinese opera she portrayed her emotions solely through the movement of her eyes while everything else remained perfectly still, an incredible skill that defines a star and takes many years of practice. When she moved her head, even a bit, the little balls would fly back and forth for some time afterwards, as if projecting her angry thoughts, while her face remained stoic. I couldn't help but laugh every time.

The actors speak in exaggerated voices with the women using high pitched voices. Fighting scenes are more symbolic than realistic and include amazing acrobatics. Although neither I, nor my wife and daughters who accompanied me, understood Mandarin we had no problem following the story. We all loved the experience and came away smiling.

On our way back to the hotel I mentioned to my host Zhong Hai that the show was quite long. He told me that what we had seen was a short version for tourists! The theater I attended in Beijing was open to the sky and without heat so dress appropriately.

Another unique and interesting place in Beijing is Gaobeidian street. This street is lined with workshops specializing in reproductions of antique Chinese furniture, wood and stone carvings. You can find everything from small stone statues for your garden to, wood window carvings, hand-made furniture and more. They will even carve anything stone or wood to order. You can, for example, specify the dimensions of your window, bed or door, and they will create a carving from wood to fit it. Prices are not high considering the workmanship.

I bought painted Tibetan and Chinese cabinets, which my daughters loved and have until this day. My method for getting such large objects safely and inexpensively back home was to have them delivered to our Chinese supplier who simply included them in their next sea shipment to us.

Last but not least I recommend a visit to a traditional Chinese tea shop which can be found in Hong Kong and Taiwan as well as China. Tea shops are not as ubiquitous in Asia as they used to be, Starbucks is everywhere in Asia too and tea shops fewer than before. Nevertheless, they can be found and are definitely worth a visit for a glimpse into Chinese culture, a great place to buy gifts for back home and who knows, you might come to really appreciate Asian tea as I did.

Traditional Chinese tea shops are not fancy but often chaotic with large bags and canisters of tea stacked all over the place. That is because it is it is all about the tea rather than the atmosphere. They will have a tea stand where they will make tea so that you can try before you buy, and are happy to let you try as many different kinds as you like.

Tea tasting tea in Taipei

There are many types of tea. Each has its own unique flavor, but these do not come from additives such as chamomile, pomegranate, vanilla, etc., as in the West. Such drinks are technically infusions and not "tea" as we like to call them. Real Asian tea comes only from the leaves of the tea tree. Like wine, the different tastes of various teas comes from the soil, altitude and how they are processed. Reviewing all the available teas would require a book of its own, (and there are such books) and is not our subject here. I will just suggest a few of my favorites to give you a starting point for your visit to the tea shop. Tea can basically be divided into three categories: Green, Oolong and Black:

Green Tea is non-fermented tea, the healthiest and least caffeinated form of tea. There are dozens of green teas but the favorite in China is Dragon Well ("Long Jing") and I recommend West Lake Dragon Well ("Xi Hu Long Jing") as the best variety although I personally prefer Oolong and Black teas.

Oolong Tea is partially fermented and between a green and a black tea. You can easily recognize it because, unlike other teas, oolong leaves are rolled into little balls. Oolong is the favorite tea in Taiwan, and Taiwan makes the best oolong in the world. Taiwanese Oolong, also called "Formosa Oolong" after the old name of Taiwan Island, is much less astringent than green tea, and much more mellow and pleasant to my taste. When fresh it has an incredible sweet, rich fragrance and taste, the kind of thing you could drink every day and never get tired of. To further confuse you there are many types of Taiwanese Oolong. I recommend "high mountain" Oolong especially "Monkey Picked Tea" if you can find it. The legend (and I don't believe it is more than that) is that this tea is grown in such high inaccessible places that only monkeys are able to pick it.

Another tea I highly recommend is "Bao Zhong." Bao Zhong is somewhere between a green and an oolong. It has the sweetness of an oolong with the freshness of a green tea. Taiwanese oolongs and Bao Zhong in particular are my favorite teas.

Black Tea is fully fermented and contains more caffeine than green or oolong but still less than coffee. Fragments of Ceylon black tea leaves is what you find in your average tea bag, but real Asian tea is always whole leaf tea. In China try Pu-erh. Proper Pu-erh comes from Yunnan province and is aged underground for years giving it a unique warm, earthy taste and a dark reddish brown color. The deep earthy flavor of Pu-erh makes me think of Tibetan monks chanting the Om. Some people immediately love it while others don't. It goes well with Chinese food which is often oily and spicy or sweet.

Pu-erh has become something of a cult in China with aged Pu-erh tea at times going for thousands of dollars a pound at auction. It is often sold in the form of pressed "bricks" with a decorative pattern beautifully wrapped and packaged. In theory you are supposed to break off pieces to make tea but in reality it is often just for show and I find have found these bricks often too dried out. I recommend instead loose leaf Pu-erh. Also beware of fakes. Pu-erh became so expensive that there is now a lot of fake Pu-erh that were not properly aged, but made to appear that way using other methods. Pu-erh is not supposed to taste fresh like other teas, so just decide if you like what you taste. Another thing you can try is a newer tea called raw Pu-erh, ("Pu-erh Sheng.") It is the same Yunnan black tea but unaged and is very good in its own way.

Chinese will no sooner add milk or sugar to any of these teas than they would add mustard or ketchup and I think you too will find that unnecessary. Fresh teas have their own rich flavor and in tea *fresh is everything*. Tea loses its florals over time and you are eventually left with no flavor. With the exception of Pu-Erh, the worst fresh tea is better than the most expensive old tea. If you have only had tea bags till now, you have never had fresh tea. Tell the tea shop you want only tea from the current season, which will be either spring or autumn with Spring teas more delicate and autumn teas fuller in flavor.

Recommended reading

The Art of War by Sun Tszu. Although written over 2,000 years ago this book is considered a classic and still studied today for its' insights on military strategy. It remains equally relevant for business strategy to which it is analogous.

The Dao De Jing by Laozi. A classic philosophical work of Chinese thought.

The Analects of Confucius The other classic that must be mentioned with *The Dao De Jing*. They are often contrasted as the two most influential works in China, even if they may seem opposed, but in fact represent two aspects of the Chinese mind and culture.

Forgotten Ally: China's World War II, 1937-1945 by Rana Mitter

China's Economy: What Everyone Needs to Know by Arthur R. Kroeber

Oracle Bones by Peter Hessler. Novel

Wish Lanterns: Young lives in New China by Alec Ash

5

HONG KONG

Historical Summary

Until The Opium War in 1841, Hong Kong Island, located just off the coast of mainland China, was sparsely populated by a few farms and small fishing villages. Today property in Hong Kong is among the most expensive in the world, it is a major commercial port, the world's largest exporter, and a world financial center. How this came about is a unique and fascinating story.

Prior to the Opium War Chinese tea, porcelain, silk and other products which were all the rage in England but the English found China uninterested in buying wool, tin and other potential British exports in return. To maintain their monopoly on these coveted products the Chinese kept their production inland and a closely guarded secret. The British, together with all foreign powers were restricted to the port of Canton, and forced to pay for their Chinese imports in gold resulting in a large trade imbalance in China's favor.

However, the British did find one product that could balance their trade deficit: Opium, which they obtained from their crown colony of India. Britain now established a very lucrative triangular trade shipping British products like cotton to India, purchasing opium there and shipping it on to China, then buying tea and other Chinese products for the return voyage to England. The British government awarded the East India Company a state monopoly on this highly profitable trade.

Not only was Opium an incredibly profitable product but it created its own market as more and more Chinese became addicted to it. As opium addiction became widespread it inevitably had detrimental effects on Chinese society. Faced with a drug crisis the Chinese government tried to halt the importation of opium. The British responded by launching the Opium War which they easily won due to Britain's superior technological development at the time.

China was forced to cede Hong Kong Island to Britain for a period of 99 years to which Kowloon peninsula was added following the Second Opium War in 1860 and later the New Territories north of Kowloon as well. British trading companies like Jardine Matheson, successors to the East India Company, now set up warehouses on Hong Kong Island which they filled with opium. Chinese ships arrived from the mainland trading tea and other Chinese goods for the drug. So while the Chinese were able to save face by not having

Britain sell opium in China, Britain was able to continue selling it from their new colony just off shore in Hong Kong.

To the credit of the British they did do a great deal to develop the city into the modern metropolis it is today. However, in 1997 Britain's ninety-nine-year lease on Hong Kong ran out and she returned Hong Kong to China under an agreement that was supposed to guarantee a continuation of the democratic system that Britain had put in place in Hong Kong. The Communist government of China has gradually eroded these freedoms, imprisoning dissidents, suppressing freedom of the press and subverting the legislature. Mass protest by the people of Hong Kong and legislature against the erosion of their rights occurred in 2014 and 2019. The Chinese government suppressed these by arresting the organizers and in some cases hiring triad thugs to attack the demonstrators.

Economy

Hong Kong was not only built on free market principles but practiced a form of laissez faire, freewheeling capitalism with low taxes and little government regulation or interference in the economy. While Hong Kong began as a trading post during the colonial era she developed a strong manufacturing sector as well. The economy grew exponentially and Hong Kong became one of the four Asian tigers. At one point tiny Hong Kong's economy was almost a third the size of China's which had stagnated under communism. As China liberalized her economy Hong Kong, with her higher labor and real estate costs, found it difficult to compete in manufacturing. Being consummate survivors, the people of Hong Kong morphed into a service economy during the 1980s.

Today Hong Kong is the 35th largest economy in the world with a 2021 GDP of 373 billion dollars and a per capita GDP of $37,000. It is the 10th largest in world trade because Hong Kong is also a major transshipment point for mainland Chinese imports and exports and is now part of the Maritime Silk Road of China's Belt and Road initiative. Since the handover in 1997, mainland Chinese companies have increased their participation in H.K and now represent half of her stock exchange. Hong Kong is the most popular city for Chinese tourists and one of the most popular tourist destinations for international travelers in general.

In essence Hong Kong has come full circle. She began as a safe place where foreign companies could do business in China without being subject to Chinese laws and restrictions and that is primarily what she is again today. The wall of skyscrapers facing Hong Kong Harbor are mostly headquarters of foreign companies investing in, or trading with China. Although now part of China Hong Kong remains a "Special Administrative Region" and is allowed to operate under different economic rules than the rest of China. So while China has eroded political freedoms in Hong Kong she is wise enough not to kill the goose that laid the golden egg when it comes to Hong Kong's phenomenal economic success and her unique role as a global center of trade and finance.

Hong Kong

People

From the Taiping rebellion of the 1850s to the Chinese civil war and Communist takeover in the 1940s Hong Kong's population continually increased as refugee's fled upheavals on the mainland and refugees continued to flee China after the Communist takeover in 1949. Consequently, Hong Kong is today one of the most densely populated cities in the world with 7.5 million people. Having little land on which to expand Hong Kong has built upwards with ever taller sky scrapers which today make up its dramatic skyline.

I have a copy of an old painting in my library showing Hong Kong viewed from Kowloon peninsula in its early days. The harbor in between is busy with ships just as it is today. The offices and warehouses of the trading companies can be seen along the shore with Victoria peak and the mountains of Hong Kong Island towering behind them. Viewed from this same angle today Hong Kong is a wall of glass skyscrapers rising up right at the water's edge. These are so tall and dense that they completely block the view of the mountains of Hong Kong Island with only the tip of Victoria peak still visible.

In addition to building skyward Hong Kong has gradually reclaimed land from the Harbor, i.e., the channel between Kowloon Peninsula and Hong Kong Island. Streets that originally fronted the harbor are now inland with new streets having been built out in front of them. Many Hong Kong residents are concerned by the shrinking harbor and have protested against it. However, with land prices among the highest in the world, and the high demand for office space, the dynamic of land reclamation and the shrinking harbor seems unstoppable.

Since most of the refugees were Han Chinese from Canton, Cantonese is the predominant language. The refugees naturally sought ways to survive and prosper in their new home which was founded as a bastion of free-wheeling capitalism and the Hong Kong Chinese are even more entrepreneurial than those on the mainland. Many of the best chefs also fled there so that Hong Kong probably has the best Cantonese food in the world.

Having lived under British rule for 156 years the Chinese adopted their class consciousness but in a more ostentatious form. Social and economic status is very important to the Hong Kong Chinese, they make every effort to obtain it and flaunt it when they do. Also perhaps because of British influence, I have found the Hong Kong Chinese somewhat more aloof than those on the mainland.

Unfortunately, they did not adopt a British sense of order and continue to be typically disorderly Chinese. This tendency to color outside the lines can sometimes be an advantage in business, and in life. I was once unable to find a taxi to the airport in Hong Kong and afraid I would miss my flight. Finally, a taxi stopped to take on another passenger but when I tried to join him I was told that they were full and by law could not take me. Israel, where I lived for ten years, can be a similarly chaotic place and I asked myself what I would do under the same circumstances there. I appealed to their humanity, asking them to ignore the rule this once and save me the disaster of missing my flight and all that that involved. There was a moment of silence then everyone in the taxi smiled and waved me in saying "hurry, get in, get in" just as they would have in Israel. Do not try this in Britain, Germany or Japan. Hong Kong Chinese may have picked up some British affectations but underneath they are still warm Chinese people.

Business customs

Prior to my first trip to Asia I read a business book suggesting that it is a nice gesture to have your business cards printed in Chinese on the other side, (I don't believe this is still necessary today). On my first stop in Hong Kong I took my business cards and stepped out of my hotel onto busy Nathan Road, the main street of Kowloon. I stopped the first person I met who happened to be a young boy, and asked if he knew where I might find a printer. He asked me why and I explained that I wanted to have my business cards printed in Chinese on the other side. He said he could take care of it and asked me to give him my cards and meet me at the same spot later that day. I took a risk and gave him most of my cards.

To my relief he was back at the appointment time and handed me a nice little case inside of which I found my cards printed in Chinese on the back to which he had added gold embossing on the edges! Everyone to whom I presented the card said that the translation was excellent. So this little boy, a complete stranger whom I approached at random, saw an opportunity and made himself a profit, while performing a valuable service for me. This bold entrepreneurial spirit is what has made Hong Kong the incredible success it is. Although the city had to reinvent itself more than once, from a trading center in the 19th century, to manufacturing in the 20th century, to financial services and shipping today, Hong Kong has always landed on its feet and continued to grow and prosper.

Hotels

Grand Hyatt is an impressive hotel in modern Asian style. It is adjacent to the convention center which is especially convenient if you are visiting a trade show. It has the largest outdoor pool in Hong Kong laid out like a resort and is a perfect for relaxing after business and cooling off from Hong Kong's high humidity. The same high humidly often causes a moldy smell even in the best Hong Kong hotels. Simply ask to change rooms, they always seem to have others without the smell. The rooms facing Hong Kong harbor are more expensive but can be very noisy due to the never ending construction extending Hong Kong into the harbor. On one visit a massive machine was pounding posts into the seabed opposite my room. I switched to the less expensive, quieter room on the other side of the hall facing the pool, and suggest you do likewise. Their Cantonese restaurant: *1 Harbor Road* is the best I've ever experience and, whether or not I stayed at the Hyatt, I went there every time I was in Hong Kong. Not only the food but the view is also spectacular. The entire restaurant has two floor high glass walls facing Hong Harbor and the lights of Kowloon on the other side.

Grand Hyatt Hong Kong
1 Harbour Road, Wan Chai, Hong Kong
Website: https://www.hyatt.com/en-US/hotel/china/
grand-hyatt-hong-kong/hkggh?src=
corp_lclb_gmb_seo_hkggh

Renaissance A less expensive, and not much worse, alternative to The Grand Hyatt Hong Kong. Renaissance is right next door to the Hyatt and shares the same views and great pool.

Renaissance Hong Kong Harbour View Hotel
1 Harbour Road, Wan Chai, Hong Kong
Website: https://www.marriott.com/en-us/hotels/
hkghv-renaissance-hong-kong-harbour-view-hotel/
overview/

Shangri-La is an elegant Asian style hotel with a nice outdoor pool. It is located near central Hong Kong on top of the large Pacific Place shopping mall. Great views of Hong Kong if your room faces the Harbor or from the restaurants on top. An outstanding feature of the hotel is the largest in the world, 16 floor high, silk mural painted in traditional Chinese style. It took 40 artists six months to create it and is worth seeing even if you are not staying at the Shangri-La. To do so take the elevator to the 34th floor atrium which will place you at the bottom of the mural. You can now take another, glass elevator opposite the mural up and down 16 floors and watch the landscape of China unfold before you.

Island Shangri-La (not the same as the Kowloon Shangri-La which is also a good choice if you want to stay on the Kowloon side).

Island Shangri-La
Pacific Place, Supreme Court Road, Central, Hong Kong
Email: hongkong@shangri-la.com
Website: www.shangri-la.com/hongkong/
islandshangrila/

Free Time

Every night Hong Kong puts on an amazing fireworks and light show unlike any you will see anywhere else. Hong Kong Harbor, the strip of ocean between Hong Kong Island and the Kowloon Peninsula, is by itself a dramatic scene with everything from junks to container ships against a backdrop of very tall modern office towers on the other side. During the nightly show every building facing the Harbor is lit up with changing multi-colored lights and moving beams of light projected into the sky all choreographed to music. It's something like the light show at the Bellagio fountain in Las Vegas except on the scale of an entire city, (at the same time, they shoot spectacular fireworks over Hong Kong Harbor).

If your hotel room or restaurant faces the harbor you can see it from the window but it is best viewed and heard outside from the park that runs along the harbor in Kowloon. The show is free and can be viewed from the Hong Kong side as well but is most impressive viewed from the Kowloon side against the towers of Hong Kong.

If you are staying on the Hong Kong side just take the Star Ferry across which is an event in itself. The Star Ferries connect Hong Kong and Kowloon and have been run continually from the beginning of the former British colony. The view of the harbor surrounded by skyscrapers is well worth the very inexpensive ticket and one of the best ways to experience old Hong Kong.

Hong Kong side of the harbor from the Star Ferry

Once in Kowloon another way to experience old Hong Kong is afternoon tea in the lobby of the Peninsula Hotel. The hotel itself was built during the British colonial period and still feels that way. Out front you will see a fleet of Rolls Royces used to shuttle guests. Tea is served in the elegant colonial style lobby with ornate high ceilings and large tropical plants throughout. It comes with a three tiered tray containing tea sandwiches, scones, and pastries, and is actually a light meal. I took my younger daughter Sivan while in Hong Kong and she loved it.

If you are like me and enjoy Maritime museums Hong Kong has one of the best I've ever visited. It contains a large collection including huge model ships from Chinese Pirate junks, Portuguese galleons, WWII battle ships, to the modern container ships that fill

Hong Kong Harbor today. There are explanations of everything along with panoramic paintings of historic views of famous Chinese harbors and sea battles.

If you stay over a weekend and have already explored Hong Kong I recommend Macau for a day, or overnight trip. Macau was colonized by the Portuguese and therefore very different feel from the former British colony of Hong Kong. Unlike the British in Hong Kong the Portuguese apparently mixed with the Chinese over their 500 years in Macau resulting in an exotic looking people with an Iberian warmth.

Unless you are there for the gambling skip Taipa Island which is a soulless collection of some of the same casinos as Las Vegas but without the glitz of the Vegas strip. In other words: It is really just for gamblers. Stay instead in old Macau. It is a charming combination of Iberian architecture and plazas, together with tropical parks, interesting sights, stores and restaurants. I never had Portuguese food before and had no idea how good it is! For a treat get yourself one of the delicious little Portuguese custard pies that are the specialty of Macau. Take a walking tour on tape from the tourist office which makes your walk around the city far more interesting while allowing you to go at your own pace and stop wherever you wish.

Macau

Macau also has a small, but very nice, maritime museum. The museum is located on the spot of the fishing village on which Macau was founded. Right next door is the original village's A-Ma Temple dedicated to the Chinese sea goddess Mazu. I was unaware of the Temple but by wonderful coincidence I happened to visit the maritime museum on the very day of the annual celebration in tribute to the goddess. It was an unexpected and amazing experience, like walking into the distant past. People dressed in incredible Chinese costumes with maritime themes paraded out of the temple and to the edge of sea on which it was built while the sound of Chinese music and the smoke and scent of incense filled the air. The elaborate ceremony culminated in the sea goddess Mazu herself being carried on a litter out of the temple and to the sea.

Recommended reading

Noble House by James Clavell. Nobel House is a historical novel about a rivalry between two British trading companies involved in the establishment and growth of Hong Kong. One of these companies (the "Noble House") is based on Jardine Matheson which remains prominent in Hong Kong today and owns the Mandarin Oriental hotel chain and other major companies. Their rival is a fictitious amalgam of various competitive British trading companies. Although a novel you will learn a great deal about Hong Kong's history, culture, people and business. On top of that it is a terrific read.

The world of Suzie Wong by Richard Mason is a classic look at the underside of Hong Kong during British rule in the 1950's and was also made into a movie. Although the main characters are a British expatriate and the Chinese prostitute he falls in love with this is not a romance novel but a very well written and a touching story with great characters you will remember forever.

A Modern History of Hong Kong by Steve Tsang

Myself a Madarin by Austin Coates. Memoires of a British Colonial official.

6

JAPAN

Historical Summary

The original inhabitants of Japan are thought to have been Asians who migrated to the Island in the Paleolithic period. For tens of thousands of years, they lived largely in isolation from the mainland as a result of which they developed unique characteristics as a people.

The country was divided into 100 kingdoms ultimately united under the Yamato court during the 4th Century AD. At this time Japan also began engaging with China and Korea and assimilating elements of Chinese technology and culture including the Chinese script and Confucian literature. Buddhism began to be introduced to the country in the 6th century. At the end of the 9th century Japan cut off relations with the Tang dynasty of China which had greatly influenced Japanese culture and Japan concentrated on developing its own unique culture, literature, art and forms of Buddhism.

The Imperial family ruled Japan as a central government taxing the people heavily while living luxuriously on the income. Unhappy with this state of affairs other members of the lower aristocracy set themselves up as local rulers and created large armies, thus beginning the Samurai era. Rivals at the imperial court began calling on various Samurai armies in their struggles for power. Eventually one of these Samurai clans, the Minamoto won out, and became the real power behind the throne. At the end of the 12th century a military government known as the Shogunate, was established by Minamoto Yoritomo. He appointed regional Shogun (military vassals) to recruit soldiers, collect taxes and keep pubic order.

The timing of this new military government turned out to be fortuitous for Japan for soon thereafter, in 1247, the Mongols, who had recently conquered most of Asia including China and Korea, launched a large seaborne invasion of 40,000 men against Japan. The Shogunate quickly mobilized a defense which was aided by a typhoon that destroyed the 200 ship invasion force. This typhoon was considered by the Japanese to be an act of divine salvation and became known as Kamikaze (divine wind).

In 1281 the Mongols organized an even larger invasion force of 140,000 soldiers. The Shogunate had spent years preparing for such an invasion and once again a typhoon destroyed the invasion fleet and the enemy was destroyed. The Japanese cut off all contact with China until the 14th century and now viewed themselves as a divinely protected people.

The Shogunate remained Japan's form of government for 700 years until the Mejii restoration of imperial rule in 1868. At the same time Zen Buddhism began to spread along with its related shoin architectural style and gardens, flower arrangements and tea ceremony. This sparse, understated, peaceful style is still apparent in Japanese design today.

The various Shogun and their sub vassals were constantly at war with each other and Japan developed as a martial culture. In 1603 the Shogun Tokugawa Ieyasu gained control of the entire country and established the Tokugawa Shogunate based in Edo which ruled until 1867. The Tokagawa Shogunate codified Shogunate control into law. A hierarchical feudal system was organized encompassing everyone's role down to the individual farmer. The Shogunate owned one-fourth of the land of the entire country directly with the remainder in the hands of local daimyo vassals and sub vassals. Loyalty towards one's superior became the highest value and this respect for authority still runs throughout Japanese culture.

The Shogunate also had a monopoly on the issuing currency and on foreign trade. Anxious to profit from trade Tokugawa Ieyasu at first tolerated the Christian missionaries who arrived with the Portuguese. He later changed policy however, and issues decrees prohibiting Christianity and requiring every citizen to register with a Buddhist temple. Following a failed Christian revolt, Ieyasu's successors increased persecution of the Christians with the goal of eliminating them from the country entirely. The Shogunate now decided to keep foreign influences out of Japan altogether and closed Japan off from the world. In 1639 Portuguese ships were forbidden to visit Japan and Japanese were forbidden from traveling overseas. Only the Chinese and Dutch were allowed to continue to trade but restricted to the Island of Dejima off Nagasaki and the new policy of seclusion was complete.

Although these restrictions were ultimately lifted centuries later the impact of this long period of isolation from the world profoundly influenced Japan which, in some ways, remains chauvinistic and relatively insular to this day. The Tokugawa system provided Japan with 300 years of peace, prosperity and a flourishing of the arts. However, it also calcified its feudal system delaying Japan's entry into the modern world.

With increased prosperity towns and cities grew and the population became increasingly urbanized. A merchant class, although despised, became increasingly wealthy along with a minority of farmers. Meanwhile the Samurai who were on top of the social hierarchy and the majority of farmers became impoverished as rice was no longer the source of all wealth. All attempts by the Shogunate to reform from the top down ultimately failed to mitigate the underlying economic dislocation. Peasant revolts against taxes they could no longer afford became frequent. Finally, a famine brought about by crop failures culminated in mass revolts in the 1830s.

At the same time Japan was coming under increasing pressure from Russia in the North and European navies in the south to open herself to trade. The Shogunate continued to resist all such attempts until a squadron of U.S. warships commanded by Commodore Matthew C. Perry entered Uraga Bay in 1853. The Shogunate finally relented and signed treaties opening Japan. This was seen by many as an abrogation of the Shogunate's primary duty and source of legitimacy as protecting Japan from the barbarians. The Shogunate was forced to make concessions to foreign powers on the one hand and the anti-foreign forces led by many of the Shogun on the other, resulting in both sides viewing it as indecisive.

During all the centuries of Shogunate rule the Imperial family remained figureheads in Kyoto but were still held in great esteem by the people. The anti-foreign forces now took up the slogan "Revere the emperor! Expel the barbarians!" After a series of defeats, the Shogunate was finally overthrown in 1868 and Imperial power restored. The Imperial family, under a young new Emperor, moved into the Tokugawa castle in Edo and renamed the city Tokyo. What became known as the Meiji Restoration was more than just a change in leadership, it was a social and political revolution which ultimately transformed Japan and brought her into the modern world. The feudal system was dismantled, the Samurai's privileges abolished, and the country completely reorganized along European lines.

Made painfully aware of Japan's technological backwardness and military inferiority by the unequal foreign treaties imposed upon her the new Japanese government instituted a program of rapid industrialization and military modernization. This was organized through private financial conglomerates ("zaibatsu") dominated by individuals connected to the court some of them Samurai. Former Zaibatsu like Mitsui and Mitsubishi remain powerful in the Japanese economy today.

The government realized that a modern state would require an educated populace and instituted universal education. This education aimed to create national unity by stressing loyalty to the Emperor and Shinto, Japan's ancient pre-Buddhist religion was elevated as the national religion. A parliament, the *Diet* was formed and a constitution created in 1889. Both received their authority from the Emperor who maintained ultimate power.

The overarching goal of all these reforms was to end the unequal treaties and achieve parity with the West which was achieved in 1894. Japan now began a campaign of conquest beginning with the Sino-Japanese war in 1895 over Korea. After defeating China, Japan forced her to sign the very sort of unequal treaty Japan had just freed herself from. Korea now turned to Russia for protection. In the Russo-Japanese war that followed (1904-05) Japan stunned the world when, for the first time in modern history, an Asia country defeated a European power.

After WWI in which the Japanese sided with the allies, Japan was treated as an equal and signed the "Four-Power Pact" with the U.S., Britain and France.

While Japan now had a parliamentary system of government the parties were dominated by the zaibatsu whose corrupt politicians passed laws in line with their own interests, and enriched themselves. This was seen as "un-Japanese" by average Japanese farmers and workers.

At the same time many junior army officers were chaffing under restrictions on the Japanese military's expansion under the "Four-Power Pact" and other treaties with the West. From these disenfranchised groups ultra-nationalist parties arose calling for a purification of Japan from Western influence. Due to Japan's small land area and rapidly increasing population she was no longer self-sufficient and these same groups also preached external expansion to insure food and other essential supplies.

The Army, without government approval, now proceeded to occupy Manchuria. Prominent business and political leaders were assassinated by the nationalists. The army enjoyed wide public support and the new young Emperor Hirohito and his court did not intervene for fear their own position would be compromised. Japan now expanded her control from Manchuria to much of the rest of China and signed the Tripartite Pact aligning her with Fascist Italy and Nazi Germany although relations with them never became close.

Negotiations with the United States over the Pacific failed to achieve results and the U.S. cut off oil to Japan. The Japanese prime minister, who had lead the negotiations, was replaced by General Tojo Hideki who now launched a campaign of conquest in Asia and the Pacific aimed at securing oil and other raw materials. War with the U.S. seemed inevitable and Japan began preparing for the attack on Pearl Harbor. The course of the War in the Pacific is well known leading ultimately to Japan's surrender in 1945.

As head of the occupation General Douglas transformed Japan into an ally of the United States and she has remained one of her most reliable allies. The Emperor was retained but only as a figurehead, a new constitution introduced and Japan became a genuine representative democracy. As a result of MacArthur's enlightened policies the Japanese not only accepted U.S. occupation but embraced it, along with American culture. Japanese militarism became a thing of the past. Having achieved its purpose in pacifying Japan the military occupation finally ended in 1958.

Economy

MacArthur had originally planned to eliminate the Zaibatsu conglomerates for their role in the war but found it necessary to leave most in place in order to aid in Japan's economic recovery. Eventually these were replaced by the "keiretsu" which are business alliances centered around a bank in which there is cross shareholding and mutual cooperation. Keiretsu companies are loyal to each other as suppliers and customers and their employees are loyal to their company. Lifetime employment within a single firm is common in Japan although this is changing and young people now change jobs more often than their parents did.

Japan's ambitions were now directed into export rather than conquest. Japan's post war economic "miracle" made Japan's economy, at one point, the 2nd largest in the world. Keys to this success was the incredible work ethic of the Japanese, Japan's early adoption of quality manufacturing principles originally developed by William Edwards Deming of the United States, and high rates of spending on R&D (Research and Development). Today Japanese industry, along with her infrastructure and transportation is among the most sophisticated in the world and her GDP of 5.2 Trillion dollars is the world's third largest after the U.S. and China. Japan's per capita GDP is approximately $40,000.

The chink in the armor of the Japanese economy has always been her complete dependence on imported raw materials and energy as Japan has very few natural resources. Japan's attempt to secure these through conquest is the underlying rationale for her expansion in Asia and the Pacific which led to war with the United States. Following the 2011 Fukushima nuclear disaster Japan shut down all of her nuclear plants making her once more totally dependent on imported energy.

People

On my first visit to Japan, one October, I was surprised to find Japanese department stores decorated for Halloween and you can see similar emulation of Western holidays on Valentine's Day and Christmas. I've seen numerous Japanese weddings on my trips to Hawaii, (the Japanese love Hawaii), always Western style. Yet, only about 1% of Japanese are Christian and the great majority identify as Shinto and/or, Buddhist and participate in those festivals as well. What you need to realize is that while the Japanese today are extremely imitative of American popular culture on the surface, in important ways they remain uniquely, wonderfully, Japanese.

Japanese are by nature shy, polite, and seek to avoid conflict at all costs. They are also more conservative than Americans or other Asians. Japanese culture is among the most refined in the world and anyone familiar with it cannot help but admire it. The Japanese retain many outstanding traditional virtues among which are honesty, humility, sensitivity and perfectionism. They take these virtues to such an extreme that many Westerners find the Japanese hard to fathom. I readily admit that I find the Japanese more difficult to read than any other people as they do not wear their emotion on their sleeve nevertheless, I have become a great admirer of their culture.

If you ask a Japanese to point the way to something he will not merely point, which he would consider impolite, but stand in front of you lift both hands palms up and move his hands in the direction you need to go walking with you and continuing to do this until you get there.

As I often did when traveling, one evening in Japan, I went to a local gym. After paying the fee for an out of town guest I was told that that I would need to wear their uniform and warm up with an instructor before using the weights. I explained that I had brought my own workout clothes and, having lifted weights for many years, I knew how to warm up, but they insisted that I wear the uniform and do an official warm up with their instructor. The instructor indicated I should follow her lead as she did a few jumping jacks and other calisthenics. When she was done I headed towards the weights but she came running after me shouting "don't throw them around." I promised not to.

Unable to find a decline bench I brought two dumbbells over to the sit up bench. In the U.S. it is common to make due with whatever equipment is available. The staff again came running over shouting: "Noooo." That bench was for sit-ups!

Careful not to violate any more rules I completed my routine and headed to the locker room to shower and change. Standing completely naked facing my locker I was surprised to hear a woman's voice just behind me. She casually struck up a conversation asking if I was an American, where in the U.S. I was from and telling me about her son who was studying in America. You are probably wondering, as was I, how in a culture that so values rules and enforces borders, a woman was in the men's locker room casually speaking to a strange naked man. However, by this time I knew enough about Japanese culture to hazard an educated guess.

There is a dichotomy central to Japanese culture. It comes, in part from the fact that Japan is a very crowded country, 125 million people in an area the size of California, that traditionally lived in houses made of wood and paper. You might well overhear your neighbors having an argument but you would *never* mention it the next day. It would be as if it hadn't happened thereby preserving privacy. The woman in the locker was a cleaning woman so her job required her to be in the men's locker room. I feel certain she would never mention our encounter outside that setting, even to me, even if nobody else was listening. It would be, for all practical purposes, as if it never happened.

My longtime Japanese business friend once explained to me that on showing a guest into one's home it is traditional to say, "welcome to my dirty house." This encapsulates the esteem with which humility is held in Japan. American style bravado will not make a good impression on your Japanese business partner.

Humor does always not translate well, in particular, American style sarcasm will be misunderstood and should be avoided. A joke at someone else's expense or making fun of someone to lighten the mood makes no sense in Asia and will destroy a relationship. Like bad mouthing others these will mark you as a crude person.

Another outstanding feature of the Japanese is their honesty. I have traveled all over the world and have never met a more honest people. My father, who also did business in Japan as Quality Control Manager for North American Phillips Corporation, once told me a story that illustrates just how incredibly honest the Japanese are. At his hotel in Tokyo he met a violinist who had forgotten a very valuable Stradivarius violin in a phone booth. Since all Japanese phone booths looked similar he couldn't remember which it was and ran around Tokyo for two days checking each one. When he finally found the correct phone booth his priceless Stradivarius was still there! Many people must have seen it and some even used the phone but nobody touched the violin simply because it wasn't theirs. Try that in New York!

Business customs

At work there is often a military like discipline with subordinates following their boss's directives to the letter and without question: Yes, right away! Once observing a Japanese assistant respond this way I thought: "Where can I get one of those!" My assistant's answer to every request was, "why?"

The Japanese feel that society functions best when clear rules are stickily observed. They wisely know however, that while such rigidity may be necessary at work and in other situations it defies human nature to maintain it 24/7. They understand that people also need to relax and let go.

That is why many Japanese bosses go out every night with their subordinates to Karaoke bars, get drunk, loud and unruly. The whole idea of Karaoke is not how beautifully you sing but to belt it out, unashamedly, with all your heart. They do this to show their common humanity, to demonstrate that they do not consider themselves above anyone else as a person, even if hierarchy must be maintained at work. In other words, there is a time and a place for hierarchy and a time and a place for comradery. There is a time and a place for work and a time and a place to relax. There is great wisdom in this. In the words of King Solomon: "There is a time for everything, and a season for every activity under the heavens:" (Ecclesiastes 3:1).

I wrote that some Japanese businessmen go out to Karaoke bars every night after work and assure you that, for many Japanese, this is, no exaggeration. My friend once mentioned that his father, the founder of their small trading company, went out to a Karaoke bar every night with his main customer from a large Japanese electronics company. I asked "every night since when?" He replied: "Since World War II."

For a foreign company to succeed in Japan usually requires far more patience than it would elsewhere. You need strong long-term relationships and an understanding of Japanese business practices. Keeping promises, for example, on delivery times, and quality are essential.

U.S. companies view promised lead times as estimates, often best case estimate with no allowances for potential delays. For Japanese companies your lead time is a promise and missing it makes you appear unreliable and perhaps even dishonest. When exporting to our Japanese customer at Sper Scientific we would therefore always add extra time to the U.S. supplier's estimated lead time when quoting our Japanese customer plus time for shipping to us. The Japanese customer might not be thrilled with our long lead time but they knew that they could rely on it, and plan accordingly.

Likewise, quality specifications are viewed as a promise in Japan, not a best case scenario. If you claim your thermometer is accurate to ±1°C make sure that is the case, otherwise your company will again be viewed as unreliable and perhaps dishonest. At Sper Scientific we applied this Japanese business thinking for all our product specifications and customers and built our reputation on it.

It is customary on sales visits in Japan to give

customers a gift. The gift is never something expensive, which might be thought of as a bribe, but something simple. I once received a simple cotton handkerchief for example from my Japanese business partner. The humble gift however will be elaborately wrapped as it is not the gift itself which is important but the ceremony of giving, receiving and opening it that is the point. If you receive such a gift never rip it open as we would in American. Japanese take great care opening a gift, as it the act of giving and receiving the gift that matters, not the gift itself. I've heard Japanese will often rewrap the gift so that they may take it home and show it to their family as it was received.

I once purchased a teapot for friends back home. It was a simple white pot but came in a beautiful well-made wooden box. I do not know if my friends still have the teapot but many years later I was surprised to find they still had the box which they considered too nice to throw out.

We once had a customer fly from Japan just to show us that labels were not straight on the outer cartons of a U.S. product we were exporting to them. No U.S. customer would consider this important as long as the actual product and product packages were good. To the Japanese the outer carton is also part of the product and must therefore be perfect.

At the end of each year it is a Japanese business custom to personally visit each customer. This is not a sales visit but simply a visit to show the customer appreciation, and thank them for their business. This is one of those beguiling Japanese customs that achieve positive results without really costing anything. Japan is not nearly as large as the United States so it is not too difficult to physically visit each customer. While emulating this in the U.S. may be impractical I think it a nice idea to at least call and thank your customers for their business, especially if you have customers in Japan.

Everyone is familiar with the Japanese custom of bowing but it is important to know exactly how to go about it. The person of lower rank always bows lower. An employee for example bows lower to a manager. All other things being equal a woman bows lower to a man. A customer is always higher than a supplier regardless of their respective titles. As you travel around Japan people will be bowing to you all day, as you enter and leave stores, restaurants, hotels and elevators. Once I happened to leave a department store at closing time. As I descended the escalator the employees lined the up all the way down to the main floor bowing and singing a company song.

At Japanese trade shows exhibitors often post two young girls on either side of their booth whose sole job it is to bow to everyone entering and leaving the booth. I didn't know this so I would ask them questions about the products on display. Their only response was to quietly giggle while covering their mouths with their white gloved hands. I didn't see how anyone could do business that way until my Japanese business friend explained the situation to me.

Even when you speak to an actual salesperson at a Japanese trade show do not expect answers to your questions on the spot. The Japanese consider this crass.

Rather they will carefully take down your questions and contact information and reply later. This is quite different than U.S. trade shows where you have to keep your head down and surreptitiously glance at booths as you walk by avoiding eye contact for fear a salesperson will jump out and launch into his sales spiel about something you have no interest in.

Tokyo Hotels

Chinzanso Tokyo offers an oasis of serenity and Japanese culture in busy Tokyo. The elegant Hotel is surrounded by a large and beautiful Japanese garden with cherry trees that blossom in the spring, leaves that turn color in autumn and camellias that bloom in winter. The garden features waterfalls, a coy pond, a bridge, a three story pagoda, stone paths lanterns and monuments. In the midst of the garden are a restaurant and teahouse.

Hotel Chinzanso Tokyo
2-10-8 Sekiguchi, Bunkyo ku, Tokyo, 112-8667
Website: https://hotel-chinzanso-tokyo.com/contact_us/

Royal Park is a good Japanese business hotel. While there are more modern and luxurious hotels in Tokyo the advantage of the Royal Park lies in its location. The Royal Park is right in the central Nihonbashi business district and convenient for business there. More importantly it is next to the Tokyo City Air Terminal (T-CAT). T-CAT has buses directly to and from Narita and

Haneda airports. On your arrival you just walk out of the terminal and into your hotel. On departure you can check your bags right at T-CAT and avoid dragging them around the airport. Prior to 9/11/2001 you could even check in to your flight right at T-CAT but unfortunately this is no longer possible.

Royal Park Hotel
2-1-1 Nihonbashi Kakigara-cho, Chuo 103-8520
Tokyo Prefecture
Website: https://www2.rph.co.jp/

Free Time

If you want to see something interesting and uniquely Japanese head to a department store just before opening. You'll find yourself in a crowd of parents and children. Look inside and you'll notice the employees are scattered about the store and all standing perfectly still, like mannequins. The rule is they must remain like that until someone touches them. As soon as the doors open doors the children rush in and run throughout the store touching all the employees they can. The parents will of course follow which is a really clever way of getting shoppers into the store at such an early hour. No advertising necessary and at no cost to the store!

Recommended reading

Shogun by James Clavell – Clavell was a prisoner of war of the Japanese during World War II and has unique insight into the Japanese culture and mindset. Shogun is a historical novel about the Samurai era from which you can learn much that is still relevant today. I read it prior to my first visit to Japan and found it gave me valuable insights.

Japan: A Short Cultural History by George Sansom

A History of Japan by Maison and Caiger

A History of the Samurai by Jonathan Lopez-Vera

Lost Japan: Last Glimpse of Beautiful Japan by Alex Kerr. On traditional Japanese arts and culture.

Forest Bathing by Hector Garcia and Francesc Miralles

The Bells of Old Tokyo by Anna Sherman

Dogs and Demons: Tales from the Dark Side of Japan by Alex Kerr.

Japan: A Reinterpretation by Patrick Smith

Shogun's Ghost: The Dark Side of Japanese Education by Ken Schoolland

7

TAIWAN

Historical Summary

The Chinese government claims Taiwan as a historical part of China but this is not entirely accurate. The aboriginal inhabitants of the Island of Taiwan arrived over 6,000 years ago and have more in common with other Pacific Islanders than with the Chinese. While there have been waves of settlement from mainland China, and Mandarin is the primary language, the Taiwanese people have developed their own unique characteristics and Taiwan's history is also not identical with China's. For periods of time China ruled Taiwan but for long periods she did not.

Until the 16th century Taiwan was ruled by native chiefdoms and few outsiders visited the Island. In 1626 the Spanish established a base in Keelung. Fourteen years later the Dutch took control of the Island and ruled it until 1661 when Zheng Chenggong, a Ming loyalist from the mainland, conquered Taiwan and made it his base of operations. In 1683 China's Qing dynasty annexed Taiwan but ceded it to Japan in 1895 following China's defeat in the in the Sino-Japanese war.

The Japanese then ruled Taiwan until their defeat in 1945 (at the end of WWII) during which time they attempted to make Taiwan an integral part of Japan. Over 300,000 Japanese were settled on the Island, Taiwanese culture and religion were outlawed and citizens were encouraged to adopt Japanese culture. The Japanese apparently had some success in their effort at cultural assimilation as tens of thousands of Taiwanese, some volunteers, fought for Japan in WWII. Taiwanese today are therefore an ethnic mix of native Taiwanese and Chinese immigrants with additional cultural elements adopted from the Japanese and other rulers.

Following the end of WWII there was Civil War in China between the Nationalists led by Chaing Kai-shek and the Communists led by Mao Zedong. By 1949 the Communists had conquered the entire country except for Taiwan where Chaing Kai-shek fled with 2 million people including his army and various elites fleeing Communist rule, joining 6 million Taiwanese already on the Island. Chaing Kai-shek established the Republic of China (ROC) on Taiwan while the Communists established the Peoples Republic of China (PRC) on the mainland. Both regimes maintained that Taiwan was part of China while each claimed the other's territory. For all practical purposes however, Taiwan was now a separate country with its own government and a free market economy, while China became a Communist country.

For the first 38 years of its rule the Nationalist's Kuomintang (KMT) party imposed martial law and ruled Taiwan through terror suppressing all dissent. The country did however, rapidly develop its industry becoming one of the four "Asian Tigers" along with Hong Kong, South Korea, and Singapore. Yet while government remained a KMT monopoly it was the native Taiwanese who led the business community.

The United States at first considered Taiwan a lost cause and expected it to fall to the Communists. However, the U.S. began to view the ROC as an asset during the Korean and Vietnam wars and the Taiwanese economy boomed.

By the 1980s the KMT began to view itself more as a Taiwanese, rather than a Pan-Chinese government and instituted democratic reforms. In the free election of 2000 the KMT lost power to the Democratic Progressive Party which advocated declaring Taiwan independent from China. Taiwan today is ranked among the highest nations in the world on human rights and tolerance.

China will not have diplomatic relations with any country that recognizes Taiwan as an independent country so there are only 13 countries that officially maintain such relations. However most of the world continues to maintain unofficial diplomatic ties with Taiwan and continues to trade with Taiwan, as does China herself. Many Taiwanese companies have set up factories in China and there are regular non-stop flights between the two countries.

Economy

Taiwan's economy was in bad shape following the end of WWII and the Japanese occupation and her prospects looked poor. Nor was the country considered a good investment as it had few natural resources and was a dictatorship. This all began to change in the 1960s. The Taiwanese government instituted land reforms which increased agricultural production and released manpower that would later be needed during her industrialization. This was accelerated by large amounts of gold the Nationalists had brought with them from China and U.S spending during the Korean and Vietnam wars.

Like Japan, Taiwan is dependent on imports for fuel, energy and food. In order to pay for these imports Taiwan needs to export and her manufacturing is therefore export driven. Small privately owned companies started making textiles, shoes and the like and later evolved into technology manufacturing.

Small companies remain the backbone of the Taiwanese economy today which differentiates it from the economies of China, Japan, and South Korea which are dominated by large conglomerates. This has proven to be a particular advantage in the fast moving world of technology production where flexibility and innovation are key. Taiwan today is a major manufacturer of computers, peripherals, and communications technology and the world's largest producer of semiconductors with world famous companies like Acer and

Foxconn. Taiwan is also a large producer of optics, tools, steel, shipping and petrochemicals.

The ease of working with these usually individually-owned, relatively small, companies is the reason why we eventually gravitated primarily to Taiwanese suppliers at Sper Scientific. This, in addition to their honesty, product quality, and other attributes I will elaborate on in "Business Customs" below, made their value proposition hard to beat. While we could often source at slightly lower costs in China, superior Taiwanese quality, flexibility and responsiveness was usually well worth the difference.

From its beginning the PRC has threatened to annex Taiwan by force and has escalated such rhetoric under China's current President Xi who pursues an aggressive foreign policy. Nevertheless, Taiwan today remains a great place to do business with a free market economy, stable democratic government, population of 23 million, GDP of $760 Billion, and per capita GDP of $32,000.

People

Taiwan is my favorite country in Asia. It has its beautiful spots but generally it's highly industrial and somewhat chaotic. There appears to be no zoning and you will find factories everywhere, in the countryside as well as the city. Taipei, where I did most of my business, and you will likely do yours, appears to have grown haphazardly with little planning. They are now trying to retrofit it with better roads and public transportation and there is ongoing construction everywhere. Taiwan is not immaculately clean like Japan, it does not have many impressive historical sites like China, or the dramatic architecture and location of Hong Kong. Taiwan is my favorite destination in Asia because of the people.

On my first visit I took a bus from the airport to Taipei. Never having been there before and unable to read the signs which are all in Mandarin, I had no idea where to get off for my hotel. I asked the bus driver, as well as passengers around me if they could let me know when we were near the hotel. As it was a small hotel, and they may not have spoken English, nobody seemed able to help me.

Finally, a man seated behind me tapped me on the shoulder and indicated that I should follow him off the bus at the next stop. He insisted on carrying my suitcase as we walked, what turned out to be a very long distance, to the hotel. He deposited my suitcase at the entrance, turned around and went back the way he came! I have been blown away by the kindness of the Taiwanese many times since then.

The natural kindness and politeness of the Taiwanese was strengthened by a movement called "Chinese Cultural Renaissance," launched in the 1960s by the KMT in opposition to the "Cultural Revolution," in China. Whereas the "Cultural Revolution" violently eradicated traditional Chinese culture, "Chinese Cultural Renaissance," elevated Chinese language, art, music and Confucian values.

While in Taiwan I usually received multiple dinner

invitations and often had to beg off some as I had already accepted another. Many of the people I did business with I consider dear friends to this day. Family is even more important in Taiwan than elsewhere in Asia. I have been to their family weddings, and they have been to my house in Scottsdale, Arizona. They have taken me and my daughters to many interesting places and love hosting visitors. As is typical of Island people everywhere the Taiwanese are warm and welcoming. You will not meet a kinder, gentler, nicer people than the Taiwanese.

Business customs

Having lived under Japanese rule for half a century many Taiwanese received a Japanese education, spoke Japanese, and often identified to some extent with Japan. That generation continued to influence Taiwanese business culture for some time after WWII. However, seventy-five years on this is no longer the case. The post war generation of Taiwanese business people were primarily influenced by the U.S. and today by Chinese business culture as well.

Like the Japanese, Taiwanese business people are reserved and conservative but this comes more from their shy nature rather than any residual Japanese influence. Like Taiwanese generally, Taiwanese business people are also very friendly and kind. Personal relationships are extremely important to the Taiwanese, even more so than elsewhere in Asia. They are not blinded by money although they obviously aim to make a profit.

Just let them know what you seek in terms of product, price and terms of payment and the Taiwanese will try to accommodate you. They seek to please their customers and solve problems, and you will undoubtedly find them a pleasure to deal with, as I did.

China claims Taiwan is a renegade province and seeks to conquer and absorb her. The Taiwanese however, have a unique ethnicity and history and hold dear their independence as a nation and as a people. You should never refer to them as Chinese or part of China, which Taiwanese will interpret as ignorance or worse.

Taipei Hotels

Grand Hyatt A modern Asian styled business hotel adjacent to the convention center, very convenient if you are attending a trade show. The hotel has a great breakfast buffet and a rooftop outdoor pool for relaxing after a long day at the show. The Hyatt is a long walk, or short taxi ride, to Taipei 101, the tallest building in Taipei. The skyscraper is shaped like a pagoda and features a rooftop observatory, accessed by a high speed elevator. The first 6 floors make up a large shopping mall with boutiques for luxury goods including every high end watch brand.

Grand Hyatt Taipei
2, SongShou Road, Taipei, Taiwan, 110060
Email: Taipei.grand@hyatt.com
Website: https://www.hyatt.com/en-US/hotel/taiwan/
grand-hyatt-taipei/taigh?src=corp_lclb_gmb_seo_taigh

Les Suites Taipei is a boutique hotel offering a more intimate atmosphere than the impressive Hyatt. You can sometimes feel disconnected while traveling and it's nice to come back to a hotel where the staff remembers you and makes you feel at home. The lobby is set up like a living room with computers all about and where breakfast is also served. The informal, intimate setting makes it easy to meet and speak to other guests. The hotel is located in the midst of a neighborhood filled with small interesting shops and restaurants and fun to walk especially at night.

Les Suites Taipei
No 135, Section 1, Da'an Rd, Da'an District, Taipei City, Taiwan 106
Email: Info.da@suitetpe.com
Website: http://www.suitetpe.com/daan/en/

Free Time

As I mentioned above Taipei is not an especially beautiful city. At night however, it becomes a very exciting place. The streets are a riot of color, lit up with neon Chinese signs hung vertically outside the small stores that line every street. These remain open until late at night with their doors open so you can freely wander in and out. When I was young, and didn't need much sleep, I loved to walk the streets and explore the city at night, sometimes buying gifts for home, sometimes trying an exotic snack. If you want a meal just head down any of the small side streets which are lined with small local restaurants.

When Chiang Kai-shek fled the mainland he took with him 650,000 treasures of China's greatest art from the Forbidden City Palace in Beijing. A large museum outside of Taipei was built to house these and that is how it came about that the National Palace Museum of Taiwan contains the greatest collection of Chinese art in the world. As large as the museum is the collection is so vast that only 1% of it is on display at any one time. This is a great way to spend a rainy day, and if you love art it is not to be missed. The gift shop has nice replicas of all kinds of arts and crafts and these can also be found at its branch located in Taipei's airport.

Now I consider myself an entirely rational person and not the sort in any way given to mysticism but I've had three very interesting experiences with Taiwanese fortune tellers which defy reason. I will relate the first of these to you, exactly as it happened, and you can decide for yourself what to make of it.

On my first business trip to Asia a number of employees from the Taiwanese company I was meeting with invited me to dinner afterwards as often happens. When asked to suggest something authentically Taiwanese, they replied "Pizza Hut!" My new business friends were disappointed when I explained that we also had Pizza Hut in America but we did ultimately find a real Taiwanese restaurant.

After dinner they took me to visit Lungshan Temple in Taipei. This was my first visit to a Buddhist Temple which I found very atmospheric and mysterious. The courtyard and interior are filled with smoke from incense sticks left burning in sand filled bowls by visitors. Through the haze you see red and gold lanterns and decorations, brightly colored offerings of fruit and numerous gold colored statues of gods of every size. Apparently they have gods for everything. I asked my Chinese hosts if they saw these statues as gods or representations of gods. After debating among themselves the consensus seemed to be that these were representations rather than actual gods.

Lungshan Temple, Taipei.

In the outer courtyard I noticed a large series of wooden drawers and enquired as to their purpose. One of my friends demonstrated by taking two red crescent shaped objects in her hand, asking herself a question, then throwing them on the floor. You only proceed to the next step if the crescent blocks land one facing up and the other down within three tries. Once this occurred she randomly drew a numbered stick from a pot. This number corresponded to one of the drawers containing a printed slip of paper on which she found her reply (i.e. fortune).

On exiting the Temple we came upon an old Chinese fortune teller sitting at a folding table and my hosts asked if I would like her to tell my fortune. I am absolutely skeptical of such things but to be a good sport I said ok. Growing up in New York I had heard about Gypsy fortune tellers who were reputed to ask leading questions then look for their answers in your face and body language. I therefore thought I'd be a smart-ass and asked the fortune teller if I could ask the questions. To my surprise she readily agreed.

I first asked her if I was married or single, to which she immediately replied "married". Next I asked if I had children to which she said "yes". "How many," "two," "Boys or girls", "girls." I was taken aback. Not only were all her answers correct but she gave them without hesitation and hardly looked at me. True the old fortune teller did not know English and my hosts served as interpreters but this was our first meeting and they knew nothing of my personal life. It was also clear from the brevity of their exchanges that they were merely relaying my questions and her answers.

Somewhat humbled I said: "Ok tell me my fortune." The old woman took my hand, studied my palm and said: "Prior to age 32 you will struggle but after that your business will take off and you will ultimately become very prosperous." Because I looked much younger than my age she assumed this was all in the future but in fact this is exactly what had happened a few years earlier at the age of 32. Nor would a stranger normally assume that I owned my own business, was already married and had two children, as I looked like a kid myself.

I now asked her one final question. I had lived in Israel for 10 years and originally returned to the United States to start a business importing Israeli products. I had planned to return to Israel after a year or so but it hadn't worked out that way. After much struggle the business was finally profitable but ultimately with European and Asian, rather than the Israeli suppliers I started out with. So I asked her if I would ever live in Israel again. I wasn't sure she even knew where, or what, Israel was but she immediately replied: "You will visit Israel many, many, times but you will never live there again." This remained true for many decades but I do now live in Israel again part time.

By this time a group of Taiwanese children had gathered around, surprised at the unusual sight of a Westerner with a Chinese fortune teller. As I began to leave they ran after me asking "Do you believe in

Chinese fortune teller?" to which I replied only half-jokingly: "I do now."

I had two other encounters with fortune tellers in subsequent years. One with a supplier who had his fortune told in Taipei and again when my daughter Keren visited and we had her fortune told in H.K. In both cases the fortune tellers' predictions came true.

Recommended reading

Taiwan A New History by Murray A. Rubinstein

Forbidden Nation: A History of Taiwan by Jonathan Manthorpe

Accidental State: Chiang Kai-Shek, the United States, and the Making of Taiwan by Hsiao-ting Lin.

Scales of Injustice by Loa Ho. On the Japanese occupation.

Hunter School by Sakinu Ahronglong Memories of an aboriginal Taiwanese.

Indigenous Writers of Taiwan: An Anthology of Stories, Essays, and Poems by John Balcom

The Stolen Bicycle by Wu Ming-yi. Novel

Taroko Gorge - Jacob Rittari. Novel

CLOSING

I hope you have enjoyed reading this book as much as I enjoyed writing it. More importantly I hope that learning from my experience will serve as a shortcut on your road to success. I have no doubt that reading this book has given you a competitive advantage over someone arriving in Asia with no previous knowledge or experience.

You now, at least, start off with an understanding of the basic concepts of doing business in Asia to which you will of course add your own interesting adventures and observations. In this sense I envy you. Discovering Asia through business has been, for me, a wonderful, enlightening experience as I am sure it will be for you too.

If you can go beyond merely understanding Asian business culture to admiring it, learning from it, and applying the best aspects of it to your own business you will have an advantage over even many seasoned foreigners doing business in Asia.

PLEASE CONSIDER LEAVING A REVIEW

If you enjoyed reading "Doing business with Asia" and found it useful please consider leaving a review. I value your honest opinion and promise to read it. Just a line or two is fine and would mean a lot to me, or make it as detailed as you like. Other readers will also appreciate your review as it help them choose books they may like.

ABOUT THE AUTHOR

DEVIN SPER is the founder and former President of Sper Scientific Ltd., an importer and distributor of environmental measurement instruments located in Scottsdale Arizona. Mr. Sper began the company from scratch in 1982, and built it into a well-known and respected brand of scientific instruments. During his 39 years as President of the company Mr. Sper traveled extensively throughout Asia developing many close business relationships and friendships. He is the author of two books and numerous articles and has been the subject of many radio and TV interviews. In 2021 he sold Sper Scientific and is now busy writing and traveling among other pursuits.

Printed in Great Britain
by Amazon